...She was a birdlike Navajo woman spry and smiling, her hair woven into a salt-and-pepper braid. "Come, come," she insisted, leading me across a flat stretch of desert to show me the exact place where I was born. It was a pile of broken sticks now, but once it had been a three-sided lean-to.

Aunt Despah marked a spot close to the remains of the lean-to. "We buried your umbilical cord right here." She was gripping my hand. "It was our way of connecting you to your home. It was to make sure that you would always come back to this place."

"Lost Bird" is the name that Native Americans give their missing children—daughters and sons who are taken from tribal reservations by theft or trickery. *Looking for Lost Bird* is the remarkable tale of a Navajo child adopted and raised by an affluent Jewish family who denied her nothing—except any knowledge of her roots and her heritage. It is Yvette Melanson's own story, of her search for identity and the blood ties that can never be broken.

YVETTE MELANSON was a stolen child who searched for her origins and eventually found them through the Internet. In her years as a Lost Bird, she served with honor in both the Israeli army and the United States Navy. She has now begun a new life on the Navajo Reservation in Arizona, the place where, as her people say, the wind knows her name.

CLAIRE SAFRAN is an award-winning journalist and contributor to major magazines (*McCall's, New Choices, Reader's Digest*). She is the author of *Secret Exodus*, a former editor of *Redbook* and *Coronet*, and a past president of the American Society of Journalists and Authors. The wind finds her in Connecticut.

LOOKING
FOR
LOST BIRD

A JEWISH WOMAN DISCOVERS
HER NAVAJO ROOTS

YVETTE MELANSON
WITH CLAIRE SAFRAN

Perennial
An Imprint of HarperCollins*Publishers*

First Bard paperback edition published 2000.

Reprinted in Perennial 2003.

Designed by Kellan Peck

The Library of Congress has catalogued the hardcover edition as follows:

Melanson, Yvette D.
   Looking for lost bird : a Jewish woman discovers her Navajo roots / Yvette Melanson with Claire Safran.
       p.   cm.
   "An Avon book"
   1. Melanson, Yvette D. 2. Navajo women—Arizona—Tolani Lakes Region—Biography. 3. Jewish women—New York (State)—Neponsit (New York)—Biography. 4. Adoptees—New York (State)—Neponsit (New York)—Biography. 5. Navajo Indians—Arizona—Tolani Lakes Region—Social life and customs. I. Safran, Claire. II. Title.
E99.N3 M5174   1999   98-42110
979.1'33—dc21   CIP

ISBN 0-380-79553-1 (pbk.)

    12 RRD 10 9 8

This book is dedicated to my husband, Dickie Melanson, our children, stepchildren, and my birth family.

PROLOGUE

I was a Lost Bird, as the Native Americans call their missing children. My life was part of a story that they have been telling around campfires and retelling in tipis and hogans for more than a hundred years.

The legend of Lost Bird began in the year 1890, on the 29th day of December, the Moon of the Popping Trees. The place was the flat, frozen valley of Wounded Knee, South Dakota, a desolate outpost to which Chief Big Foot had led the remnant of his people, a ragged band of Lakota Sioux men, women and children.

Cold and hungry, weary and hopeless, the Lakota had come to give themselves up to the United States Cavalry. Armed soldiers were deployed around them, and rapid-fire Gatling and Hotchkiss guns looked down on them from a nearby ridge. In the final act of surrender, the Lakota men were turning their rifles over to the blue-coated soldiers.

Suddenly, a single shot rang out, probably fired by accident, perhaps by a despairing Lakota warrior, perhaps by a nervous cavalryman. The troops were ordered to open fire, and they responded with a steady and withering barrage. The Lakota fell like grass before a relentless scythe. Witnesses said that as many as half of the men fell under the first volleys from the rapid-fire guns. Some of the women and children tried to flee the massacre, or to hide among the gullies and wind-stunted pine trees, but they were pursued and shot down. When the guns fell silent, three hundred Indians, most of them women and children, had been killed. It was, as one newspaper of the time called it, "a terrible hour's slaughter."

When it was over, as the Indians still say, "the sky wept snow." A blizzard hit, raging over the terrible scene. For three days, snow swirled and fell, smothering the valley. For three nights, the only sound was the mournful howling of the wind. Afterward, cavalry soldiers walked among the snow drifts, searching for survivors among the heaps of bodies that lay scattered across the valley and along the clay banks of Wounded Knee Creek. They thought that no one could have lived through this carnage.

Then the soldiers heard an unexpected sound. "What was that?" one man asked. They listened and heard it again—a baby's faint cry. They searched and found a Lakota baby girl, barely alive, underneath the sheltering corpse of her mother. They had to pry the child loose from her mother's frozen arms. The little girl wore a buffalo-hide cap, lovingly decorated with beadwork, and her cries grew louder as they took her away from the mother whose body had shielded her from cavalry bullets and then protected her from the snow and fierce cold.

No one knew the girl's name, and so they called her Lost Bird or Zintkala Nuni. She was adopted by one of the cavalry officers, and she grew up far from her own people, a stranger, an oddity, a lone Indian in a white world. Not much is known of her, but they say that her life was brief and tragic, and that she spent much of it searching for an Indian family whose name she never knew. Zintka, as she was sometimes called, died at only twenty-nine.

Her story was half-forgotten until, many decades later, a faded photograph was found in the bottom of an old trunk in a dusty attic. It showed an Indian baby in the arms of a general in full, gold-braided dress uniform. On the back of the photograph, in fine Victorian script, he'd written a message: "Zintkala Nuni, Lost Bird, found on the field of Wounded Knee on the fourth day after the battle . . . and adopted by me. Yours, L.W. Colby."

Zintka was traced to California by two women, Marie Not Help Him and Renee Sansom-Flood. They discovered her grave, neglected and overgrown, in a cemetery in Hanford. They whispered a prayer, and then they arranged for her body to be exhumed and brought home to the Wounded Knee Memorial. She now lies next to the mass grave where her mother was buried.

Oh, Zintka, I know you. Oh, Lost Bird, I remember you. Oh, stolen child, I am you.

Generations later, I was living my life as Zintka's descendant. I too was lost. I too was searching. From Zintka's day to this one, almost every Indian family can tell you the story of its own Lost Bird. The details may change but the heart of the story is always the same.

At the time that I was born, in 1953, and for many years afterwards, about one in four Indian children were taken from their homes and placed in non-Indian settings. It was done by bending and sometimes breaking the law of the land. It was done, white Americans said, "for the good of the child."

Some Indian families believed what they were told by the white people who ran the reservations. They allowed their young children to be loaded aboard trains and transported to distant boarding schools, where they were forbidden to speak their own language and taught to forget their own culture. Some of the children returned to their families as strangers; many never came home again.

Against their parents' will, other children were taken as infants, as eight-year-olds, as teenagers. Under the white man's law, age did not matter. The children were scooped up by social workers or missionaries who claimed their parents were "too poor" or "too ignorant," "too drunk" or "too savage" to raise their own children. Indian mothers wept as their sons and daughters were placed in orphanages or white foster homes, sometimes with a promise to bring them back in a few years, a promise that was not always kept.

And some children just disappeared, snatched in that quick moment when their mothers looked away, kidnapped as babies from where they slept in the shade of a brush arbor, or the flatbed of a wagon, or the crib of a hospital ward. Their mothers never knew what happened to them, but they were sold or given away to white couples who adopted them, often without knowing the full story of how those children came to be "available."

I was one of those stolen babies. I now have a file drawer crowded with proof that I was taken illegally from my birth parents when I was just a few days old. I was separated from my twin brother, who was also stolen, his whereabouts as hidden as my own. I was passed from person to person, like contraband that was too hot to keep. Then, when the trail had cooled and I was three years old, I was placed in adoption with Beatrice and Lawrence Silverman. I lived for some forty years without knowing who I was or where I had come from.

But I was luckier than Zintka, my sad ancestor. She came home only in death. I was still alive and finally going home. Or going to the place that people said was my home, a Navajo reservation where the faces were unfamiliar and the landscape strange. If Zintka had lived, would she have felt as I did about going home? Would she too have been going slightly crazy with confusion and questions? Who was I? Would she have asked that? Where do I belong? Would she have had an answer?

I was a woman in a hurry, as usual, driving across the country toward an unpredictable future, steering an aging black van that my husband Dickie Melanson had tinkered with and prodded into locomotion. With every mile, I was leaving an old identity behind and coming closer and closer to a new one.

"Are you sure we're doing the right thing?" I asked Dickie.

"Well, I'm surer than you are," he told me.

He sat beside me, checking maps for our current location and counting off the exits until the next interstate on our itinerary. "Dickie" was his legal name, given at birth, a too-cute name for the wry and wiry man he'd become, a name he'd kept partly out of loyalty to his mother, partly out of contrariness to the rest of the world. That day, he had two concerns. One was my unreliable inner compass; if we got lost, that raised the dread specter of having to ask someone for directions. Like most men, Dickie would sooner stand naked in K-Mart's window.

His other concern, which I shared, was speed. "Give it some gas, Yvette," he said. I was going as fast as I could, but that isn't all that fast when you're driving a patched-together van and pulling a horse-trailer crammed with some furniture and other belongings from a past life. Some of it wasn't worth the hauling, but when I packed I was feeling like Ma Joad in *The Grapes of Wrath*, a book I had read back in junior high. Moving west, she worried about having to leave behind almost everything that was familiar. She packed what she could. "How will we know who we are," she asked, "without our past?"

Good question. I have lived most of my life without much of a past and without being very certain of who I am. Maybe that's true of anyone who is adopted. But when you go looking for your true self, you don't always find what you'd expected. I was still shaky with what I'd learned about my once and future selves.

I used to be white.

I used to be Jewish.

I used to be rich.

And, as anyone could tell from my speech, I used to be from New York.

By 1996, though, I had moved to a sagging white farmhouse in Palmyra, Maine. Long ago, I had stopped being rich, but I still thought I was those other things. Then, using my computer to browse the Internet, I found an adoption forum. I clicked onto it, asked a few questions and got a few answers. I posted more questions and got more answers by e-mail and then by phone. Eventually, I learned that I was none of the above.

Driving along, I caught sight of my face in the rearview mirror. The shape of it had not changed. The color of my skin was the same as it had always been. But I was morphing into someone new, no longer the woman I used to think I was, not yet the woman I was born to be.

The only visible difference, so far, was my hair, parted in the center, hanging long and straight, with layers of color that told my history like strata on a geologic rock. The tag ends still hinted at a long-ago blond, the hair color of my childhood, recaptured as an adult, thanks to those wonderful folks at Clairol. The middle sections were auburn, the remnants of other experiments in trying to reinvent myself. The roots were dark, the real me, the emerging answer to a lifelong question.

According to the evidence, I was no longer "white," but "red," a Native American, a Navajo Indian, as full-blooded as they come. I was still Jewish. Or was I? For how long? I was no longer from New York, but from a ruined hogan on the parched plains of a Navajo reservation in Arizona. No oil wells there. No high-rolling casinos. Just a clan of strangers who said they were my long-lost family.

Like so many adoptees, I'd searched for my origins. Like so many lost children, I'd daydreamed about finding my family and meeting them. My plan was to visit them. My idea was to stay in touch and exchange occasional letters. That's what most adoptees do. But here I was, leaving behind everything familiar, drawn by something I didn't yet understand, crossing the country to move in with my unexpected family.

All the events of my life were prelude and preparation for this cross-country migration. A few years earlier, I might have made a different decision. I might have stayed put, not ready to accept the strangeness. Everything that had happened to me in my forty-rather-odd years had prepared me to start off on this journey. And nothing had prepared me for what I would find at the end of it.

My two daughters sat in the back of the van, surrounded by a litter of coloring books and paper cups of Kool-Aid. Heather, my eleven-year-old, was the one who took after her father, with a thin and angular body, with dark eyes and a mischievous smile, with his spikey hair and with the high-definition cheekbones that a fashion model would kill for. Lori, my ten-year-old, had my stockier build, my once-blond hair, my light eyes and my cheekbones, the broad, flat cheekbones that I now knew were a Navajo hallmark.

If I had a new identity, so did they. Before we left Palmyra, Lori had raced around town, spreading the news. "Guess what?" she told everyone. "I'm a half-breed!" If some people didn't see that as a badge of honor, she didn't notice.

For now, dressed in our Melanson family uniform, blue jeans and tee-shirts, she and Heather were taking it as a great adventure. "There's one!" shouted Lori, pointing at a passing car. The girls were competing to see who could spot the most license plates from Maine, the state we were leaving behind, and from Arizona, the state that would be our new home. Moving down the Atlantic seaboard, heading now into Tennessee, the sightings were few and far between.

It was now almost a year since I began to find the answers to my lifelong questions, and they had come like lightning bolts. Now I was driving down the highway toward a new life on the Indian reservation where I was born. At long last, I had found the place where I belonged. Or so I hoped. I was about to step out of my old identity, like a snake shedding its skin, and try on a new one. I was supposed to dress my five-foot-four self in a new set of facts which, frankly, I was finding hard to believe.

A Jewish Indian? It was a weird hybrid, a combination so strange that everyone who heard about it wanted to know more. Reporters came banging at my front door. My phone rang off the hook with requests for TV appearances. I said no to most of them, because I needed to understand it myself before I could explain it to other people. In the hope that it might help to find my missing brother, though, I did allow a part of my story to appear on *20/20*. In that same hope, I began to write this book.

I have made this trip from Maine to Arizona once before, by plane, at the invitation of the Navajo Nation. TV cameras from ABC and other stations were waiting for me when I landed, blinding me with their lights, rattling me with their questions. They wanted answers that I was still searching for.

On that brief trip, I found some of those answers. A tall

and weathered *shaman* or medicine man put his arms around me and told me, "You are my daughter." His embrace was like none other I'd ever known. It was all-encompassing, like being in a warm cave of love. A Navajo woman, fortyish, her skin coppery, her face like a full moon, said, "You are my sister." An older woman, a reservation auntie with a long braid down her back and a gold tooth in her mouth, showed me the sun-baked ruins of the lean-to where I was born. "You look just like your mother," she said. "You belong to this place."

Did I? That visit gave me part of the answer. Soon after my return to Maine, I received another part of it. A man in a brown United Parcel Service uniform delivered a package to my farmhouse door. The return address was that Arizona reservation, and when I opened it, I found a collection of gifts from the heart. Wrapped in tissue paper, there was the embroidered and beaded dress that I had admired on one of my sisters. Protected by cotton wool, there was the turquoise bracelet I had asked to try on. There was the blue shirt that I had told another sister was "so pretty." And there were the moccasins that I had borrowed from someone else because they felt so good on my feet.

It was a collection of the things I'd admired during my visit with my Navajo family. I do not cry easily, but the tears came that day. It was a long time since I had felt so loved, so cherished.

"Funny," people used to tell me, "you don't look Jewish." I used to scowl at that. I still do. "I'm as Jewish as anyone," I used to say. I have lived in New York neighborhoods where I thought the whole world was Jewish. And I have lived in the small town of Palmyra, Maine, where I was a minority of one. "I am who I am," I used to tell myself. But driving along, I wondered who in the world that was.

At the Tennessee state line, we stopped for gas and a

coffee break. The waitress was feeling chatty. She noticed
my moccasins and asked about them. We talked for a while.
"Funny," she said. "You don't look Indian."

I smiled and gave a little shrug. Looks are deceiving.
Back in the van, we joined the traffic that was veering west,
following directions, bumper to bumper with destiny. Who
am I? Who hasn't asked that question? Some of the answers
come from the rearview mirror. Some lie ahead in the chap-
ters that I'm about to live.

CHAPTER 1

She was a birdlike Navajo woman, spry and smiling, her hair pulled back from her face and woven into a salt-and-pepper braid. She was dressed in a long skirt of black velveteen, high fashion for reservation aunties. I met her on my first trip to Arizona, when newspaper and television reports were spreading the word about a Jewish woman who was really an Indian. In that moment, I was still full of doubts and questions, still fighting the idea that I might be an Indian, still unsure of what that might mean. At that point, everything I knew about Indians had been learned from John Wayne movies.

I had so many questions, so much to learn, so much to catch up on.

The president of the Navajo Nation, the largest of the surviving Indian nations, had been told about me and had checked the evidence. He'd invited me to come to Arizona with Dickie and the girls, to be welcomed back into the tribe, to meet my Navajo family and then to be flown back to Maine—all in two dizzying weeks.

The woman smiled, showing a gold tooth that glinted in the sun. She told me to call her Aunt Despah and then, on the fourth day of my visit, she pulled me away from the rest of the relatives who had gathered at the ruins of the old family ranch.

"Come, come," she insisted. Clutching my hand, she led me across a flat stretch of desert to show me the exact place where I was born. It was a pile of broken sticks now, but once it had been a three-sided lean-to set at the edge of a cornfield.

My mother had been harvesting ears of blue corn when the labor pains began. They came too suddenly, too quickly for her to walk the mile back to her home. Instead, Despah, my mother's kid sister, helped her to the shelter of the lean-to. My father found them there and then, spurring his horse, rode off to get Aunt Carrie, my mother's older sister.

By the time they returned, the pains were coming sharper and closer together. Helped by her sisters, my mother was standing up, in the old Navajo style of child-birth. She held tightly to the main support of the lean-to, an upright railroad tie, hoping that gravity would be her friend. My father waited outside, chanting prayers and keeping an eye on the two little daughters who had been with my mother.

Finally, I was born. Her sisters told my mother to lie down and rest, but she shook her head; she felt another life within her. A short time later, as Despah remembered, my brother was born. It was the first twin birth that anyone could recall in Tolani Lake.

"Your brother was dark, like most of us, with a small birthmark on the left side of his face," Aunt Despah told me. "You were white, very white, with a birthmark on the middle finger of your left hand, and another one on your foot." I had never given much thought to those two dark circles, which I always thought of as "beauty marks," but they are still there.

Aunt Despah marked a spot close to the remains of the lean-to. "Right here," she said. "We buried your umbilical cord right here." She was gripping my hand. "It was our way of connecting you to your home. It was to make sure that you would always come back to this place."

Something stirred within me. Flesh and blood. Powerful symbols. Scientists think that migratory birds find their way across thousands of miles by instinct, following the gravity pull of the North and South Poles. And Lost Birds like me? Are we drawn by a different gravity, a guidance system of our own?

Now, mile after mile, driving west in an uncertain van, I felt the tug. I was being pulled toward a strange land that everyone said was my home. This second trip was not just a visit. My daughters thought of it as a great adventure, but it was more than that too. It was a leap into the unknown, and it was supposed to be forever.

For as long as the grass shall grow? Is that what Indians would say? I was moving bag and baggage, heart and soul, husband and children. *Oy vey*, as my Jewish family used to say. *Oy gevalt*.

I concentrated on getting ready. All of my forty-three years, I have been a hard-headed woman, stubborn and logical, wanting a reason for everything. "Seeing is believing," I used to say. Navaios too are logical, but in a different way. For them, it begins by turning that old aphorism on its head. Believing, they kept telling me, is seeing.

That's what I was struggling to do. This trip was my Vision Quest. If things had been different, if I hadn't been stolen from my mother's arms, I might have made a Vision Quest as a teenager or a young adult. Over time, I might have made more than one. By tradition, I might have gone into the mountains, spending as long as four days in soli-

tude, making do without food or shelter, fasting and medi-
tating to connect with my inner spirit and with a vision of
my deepest self.

Instead, I was doing it in a van, on the interstate. I had
food and water but, traveling both by day and by night, not
much sleep. I was in the middle of my crash course on who
Indians were and who, therefore, I might be.

By now, I knew enough to get started. I'd grown up
going to Passover seders and asking the famous Four Questions. "How is this night," I would begin, "different from
all other nights?" The answers were always right there, in
the book in front of me. Now I was looking for other answers, still elusive, still unknown, still unwritten. I was focusing my mind on the three sets of questions that you're
supposed to ask during a Vision Quest.

First, who am I? With what do I identify? With whom?

Secondly, what have I become with the who that I am?

And thirdly, why am I here? What is my purpose?

Good questions. Hard questions. And first questions
first.

I was born a twin, a special blessing, a sacred thing
among the Navajos. In the beginning, as the Navajos tell it,
when the First Beings emerged from under the earth, there
was Changing Woman, who was herself born of darkness
and dawn. Her children, the Twin Hero Gods, made the
world safe for the *Dineh*, or the People, as the Navajos still
call themselves, by ridding the earth of the terrible monsters
that threatened human life. The Twin Heroes fought and
killed the monsters with bows and arrows, and the arrows
were made of lightning.

The Navajos also believe that the Holy People—unseen
beings, a little like saints, a little like angels, helpers and
agents of the Great Spirit or the One God—are twins. And
so human twins are thought to have special powers. I felt a
twinge of regret when I first heard about that. "Oh, if only

I'd known . . ." I thought. There were so many times in my life when a secret, special power was just what I needed—but didn't have.

My brother and I were a difficult birth, exhausting my mother. They carried her back to her home, a hogan or small hut made of logs and covered with mud and twigs. It was round, a sacred shape among the Navajos. If you stand in a circle, you are united with everyone else who is within it. A circle is outside of time, with no beginning and no end.

By tradition, the entrance to the hogan had faced east, toward the rising sun. In that strange and barren landscape, there was a click of recognition. In my life as a Jew, I too had faced east—praying toward Jerusalem.

When she awoke the next morning, my mother could see that something was wrong. As my father has since told me, as Despah and Carrie remembered, my white skin was turning yellow, with tinges of blue on the lips and fingertips, and I could not keep down my mother's milk. My father was a Navajo medicine man, but he did not try to heal me with sacred songs and holy chants. Navajos believe in modern medicine for physical ills; they use their own medicine for ailments that penicillin can't cure, afflictions that are emotional or spiritual, or problems that are supernatural, brought on by the sins of one's past or by witchcraft and other curses.

Instead, my father hitched his horse to a borrowed wagon and took his wife and new babies to the trading post. There, the white who ran the trading post helped them into his truck and drove them to the nearest hospital, fifty miles away in the little town of Winslow. Years later, I recognized the name of the town. I grew up singing along to "Take It Easy," a hit song by The Eagles, and I always remembered the line that went: "Standin' on the corner, in Winslow, Arizona . . ."

At the hospital, my parents were told to leave both children, though only one of us needed medical attention. My parents may have been puzzled by that, but in those days, Indians tended to do as they were told. Today, Navajos govern themselves, but back then they were humble. Back then, they'd forgotten much of their own wisdom and strength. White people held all the power and, as they never hesitated to tell the Indians, they knew best.

My brother and I were left at the hospital. My mother stayed overnight, and was then sent home. As a nurse explained to my parents, the hospital would get in touch when both children were well enough to go home.

A week passed without any word, and my parents traveled again to Winslow. The twins were no longer there. "Taken to the hospital in Fort Defiance," my parents were told. They traveled to that town and asked for the children. "I want my babies," my mother kept saying to the doctors. "Where are my babies?" She was told that they were fine, but that she'd have to come back some other time to see them. A few days later, my parents traveled once again to Fort Defiance, but the twins were no longer there. Maybe we had never been there. My father has come to think that it was a runaround. He has come to suspect that we were spirited away on that first day in that first hospital.

My mother could not stop weeping. "Where are my babies?" she kept asking. Her tears haunt me. Her question was destined to be my own. I grew up far from my mother, in a world that was white, but it did not save me from repeating her history. I too have fought and argued with officials who held all the power, people who lied, bureaucrats who seemed to speak a different language. I too have lost a child, a firstborn son named Brad who was pulled from my arms and taken away to live with strangers. I know what my mother must have been feeling, because I too have lived with that emptiness.

My twin brother and I had gone missing in Winslow

and, over the next several years, my mother wore out the road between that dusty town and her home on the Tolani Lake reservation, hitching rides when she could, trudging long miles on foot when she couldn't. She paced the streets and peered in the shop windows. She stared at every child she saw. She stopped strangers to ask if they'd seen her children. She never stopped looking for us, but my twin brother and I were gone like smoke, whisked away by an underground network of doctors, nurses, missionaries, and shadowy adoption arrangers.

I knew none of this, of course. I heard the story from my Navajo family when, forty-three years later, we finally found one another. Now my task was to fit that story into the one that I have always known.

In my first years, I was contraband, "hot," a stolen child who needed to be hidden and disguised. I was separated from my twin brother and, in Navajo tradition, that meant that we were in danger, stripped of the special power that belongs to twins. I was moved from place to place and passed from person to person. I must have been handled with care, since I remained intact, with no visible bruises. But now, on a quest for my inner self, I wondered about that. If I looked deep inside, what scars would I see? What would they tell me of how those unsettled years had affected the person I became?

My earliest memory is of a sense of guilt, and then terror. I was sitting cross-legged on a blue-gray rug, the only touch of color in a black-and-white memory. I was watching a pretty woman in tears. She was pacing the floor. She was wringing her hands. Trying to be still, hunching over to make myself as small as I could, I knew one thing for certain. If she was crying, it had to be my fault.

All these years later, the woman's name is lost to me, and her face is a blur. She was a kind and gentle stranger, one of a long string of people through whose hands I passed in my early years. No one seemed to keep me for very long, and I remember wondering what was wrong with me.

I was a blond child with green eyes, staring in confusion. I was three, the age of remembering, but people had already started to lie about my age. As my Navajo family has now proven to me, I was born on September 10, 1953, but someone had fiddled with my birth certificate, changing the month to August and the year to 1955.

I was sitting there on that gray-blue rug, next to a big armchair, when two strangers arrived. The man wore a rumpled business suit. The woman was in a dark dress and had her hair pulled back in a strict bun.

The pretty woman was crying harder than ever. The strange woman was bending to pick me up. "No!" I shouted. I kicked and tried to squirm away, but her strong hands were on me. My screams were wild and terrified. Why didn't the crying woman help me? Why didn't she stop this? If anyone said anything, I don't remember. All I remember are my own screams, as loud as I could make them.

And I have always been good at making loud sounds.

The strange woman placed me, still screaming, in the backseat of a car and then climbed in beside me. The man sat behind the wheel, started the car and drove off. They were taking me away, and so now I knew another thing for certain. I must have done something really bad.

In my memory, the car stopped in front of a large building. By then, I had worn myself out with screaming. The strange woman carried me into the building, entering through a foyer or reception area with a vaulted ceiling, higher than any I'd ever seen, and moving down a long, deserted corridor. I can still hear the woman's heels echoing loudly on the marbled floor. We came to a huge room with a lineup of big metal cribs, all of them empty until the woman placed me in one of them.

I slept. I woke. I slept again. Someone came to feed me with a spoon. I remember being upset, because I wasn't a baby; I knew how to feed myself. Time passed, but I was not old enough to tell how much time. Eventually, the woman with the bun on the back of her head returned. She picked me up and carried me back to the car.

We drove to a train station and got on board. I scrunched down in my seat, staring out the window, confused and scared. The woman didn't speak and didn't explain. She had a thermos of iced tea and poured some into a baby bottle for me. I remember feeling annoyed, because I knew how to drink from a cup. But if I made a face, she paid no attention. I was wearing a dress and panties, not diapers. I was potty-trained by then, but after the iced tea I had an accident. Or maybe it wasn't an accident. I can still see that woman's face, red with annoyance, as she reached into a bag and pulled out clean clothes to change me. It's called "getting even"—and it's a habit I acquired early on, a child's way of feeling less powerless, a survival technique when you're in the clutches of an overbearing adult.

For a long time, we rocked along on that train. Eventually, we came to a warm, sun-struck place that I now know was Miami Beach, Florida. We took a taxi to a building that was even bigger than the first one, a marble palace that I've since learned was the Fountainbleu Hotel. By then, the woman was letting me walk on my own, but she kept a tight hold on my hand. She led me down a hallway, through some doors and out to the pool area. Everyone was in bathing suits except for us and for one man in a shirt and trousers and a woman in a pink silk dress.

The bun woman brought me to them. They bent down, hugging me, kissing me. It scared me at first, and I started to scream again. They spoke softly to me, and they seemed so happy that I calmed down. I noticed that the bun woman had disappeared, and that seemed like a good sign.

They took me upstairs, smiling at me, touching me as if they wanted to be sure I was real. "Look at that face," the man was saying. "Have you ever seen such a pretty face?" We came to a bedroom where the woman changed my clothes, putting me into a ruffled dress. She brushed my hair, kissing me betwen every stroke of the brush. We went back downstairs to a dining room, where they let me feed myself. Another good sign. The woman called me *shayneh maydele*, which I soon learned was Yiddish for "pretty girl."

"Your name is Yvette," they told me.

I gave them a smile. I had no memory of what I was called before but, for the time being, terror was behind me. We were upstairs again, and they were putting me to bed.

"And our names," they said, "are Mom and Dad."

CHAPTER 2

What's in a name? Only a label. Only a way for people to tell who you are. Only a way to think about yourself. Yvette was Yvette, the fancy French name I had always lived with, the person I was raised to be. But who was Minnie Bob, the name I was born with, the person I should have been?

"What do you call a Jewish Indian?"

In the back of the van, my daughters had their heads together, Heather and Lori, one dark-haired, one blonde, and they were laughing, a wonderful sound for this mother's ears. We were eating up the miles, moving now through the flatlands of Texas, and my daughers were doubled over, hooting at a silly joke.

"What do you call a Jewish Indian?" Heather was asking.

"I don't know," Lori answered. "What do you call a Jewish Indian?"

"A Shmohawk!"

Not the world's greatest joke, I thought, but not bad for an eleven-year-old. Would Indians think it was funny? Or offensive? As a Jew, I had a built-in radar for which jokes were innocent and which ones were hurtful. But as a newly minted Indian, my antennae were not yet out.

"Listen to this," Lori was saying. "I've got one too." She was bouncing in her seat. "Here it goes," she said.

"What's life?"

"Okay, I'll bite," said Heather. "What's life?"

"Life is just a bowl of Cherokees."

The jokes were getting sillier. "You're going from bad to verse," I told them, tapping on a make-believe cigar, doing my Groucho Marx. My daughters' giggles were just the background noise I needed. On this makeshift Vision Quest, their laughter was one more thing for me to meditate on.

My birth mother never heard me laugh. Her name was Betty Jackson Monroe, and she was robbed of that moment, an immense loss for a Navajo mother. Christians have baptisms for newborn children, and Jews have *brises* or circumcisions for boys and naming ceremonies for girls. But, as my newfound sisters have told me, Navajos have a different ritual, a ceremony of their own for a new baby.

They wait. They watch. And they listen. They are waiting for the baby's first laugh. It has to be spontaneous and self-generated; no kitchy-kooing and no tickling allowed. It usually happens when the baby is a month or so old. And then they celebrate.

What an idea! From the minute I heard about that, I loved it. After all the new and strange things that I was struggling to understand, here was something that I grasped immediately. A baby is a great joy, and its laughter is a true blessing from whatever holy spirit you believe in.

Eyes on the road, I remembered the tradition I'd been told about. I thought of how it might have been, if I hadn't been stolen from my parents. When I laughed out loud for the first time, my older sisters would have run from hogan to hogan, issuing invitations and spreading the word. Meanwhile, my mother would have been busy cooking. She'd have taken her wedding basket, the woven basket that was used in the marriage ceremony for her and my father, the basket with a circle, endless and unifying, painted in its center. She'd have filled the basket with food—corn cakes, tortillas, blue ears of Indian corn, whatever she chose.

My mother would have propped me up on pillows and placed the basket in front of me. And then people would have arrived to accept the gifts from the basket, a symbol of the gifts that this child was bringing to this world, a hope that the life of this child would always be blessed with laughter.

No such celebration was ever held for me. No one knows where I was when I gave my first laugh. No one knows who heard it. And for Navajos, famous among Indian tribes for their wit, their good humor, their love of practical jokes, that was a cause for great sadness.

Still, in my growing-up years, far from the people whose blood ran through my veins, I did have the blessing of laughter. However I got there, I was lucky to have landed in the arms of Beatrice and Lawrence Silverman, and they heard my laughter a lot. It was loud. It was long. It often gave me the hiccups.

My adoptive parents praised and pampered me. Why wouldn't I be laughing? They gave me love, a home, a religion, and an identity. Why wouldn't I be happy? They half-convinced me that being adopted was better than just being born.

"You're special," Bea used to say. "That's why we chose you." Over and over, like a fairy tale we both wanted to be true, she told me the adoption story.

"We looked for you for a long time," she began. "We

wanted a child, but we couldn't have one. There was a great empty space in our hearts, and we longed to fill it. We wanted to be a real family. We waited and waited. We searched and searched for a child. We kept looking for the right one. And then we found you.

"We chose you," she always said, and the words were sweet and tangible, like a caress. "You were so special. The minute we saw you, we fell in love with you."

It was the standard story, the one most adopted children are told. But I didn't know that then. It was only half the story, but I still believed that the important parts were true. Searching my memory now, it was the other half of the story that nagged at me. It was the untold parts that loomed large. What secrets did Bea and Larry keep from me? How much did they know about where I came from? The questions tumbled, one after the other, in my mind. Did they know I was a stolen child? Did they know my real age? Did they know I was born an Indian?

My head ached. This business of Vision Questing was hard. It hurt to think negative thoughts about Bea, who raised me with so much love. It was painful to break a lifelong habit, making excuses for Larry, and to face the truth about the father who loved me for a while and then rejected me. Both Bea and Larry were gone now, unable to explain themselves. If there were any answers, they had to be in my memories of them.

Behind the van, in the horse trailer that we were pulling, was my most treasured possession, a framed portrait of Bea Silverman. It had hung in my childhood home and then in the living room of the old farmhouse I shared with Dickie. It showed a striking woman, dark-haired and dramatic, and it used to make Dickie uneasy. "Her eyes are always watching me," he complained. "They're always following me."

Even in a portrait, Bea was a presence you couldn't ignore. She stood five feet ten in her heels, which she never stood without. She was thirty-eight when I was adopted and, behind the drama, she was loving, gentle, and generous, just born to be someone's mother. Fate had played her a dirty trick: something was amiss with her body; three pregnancies had ended in miscarriages and a doctor's warning not to try again.

She was a college graduate and a spiritual woman, with an intense inner life. But, as she was always explaining to me, appearances counted. Every morning, she squeezed into the armor that so many women used to wear back in the fifties, an all-in-one corset that flattened her stomach, nipped her waist, and uplifted her formidable bosom. "Yvette, give me a hand," she'd ask, and I'd help to fasten the last few, hard-to-reach hooks and eyes.

Bea did not like to be caught without her makeup on and her hairdo in place. Between her weekly appointments at the beauty parlor, she slept with her hairdo wrapped in tissue paper and protected by a big, flowered cap, like a shower cap. One morning, when a visitor arrived at the door unexpectedly, catching her still in that cap, she was amazing. She kept talking. "Come in, come in. How nice to see you." She didn't miss a syllable. She just spun around and, shazam, the cap was off, the tissue paper was gone and there she was, like magic, perfectly coiffed. She spun around again, still talking. "And how's the family?" For what seemed like less than a minute, she was out of the room. And then there she was again, perfectly made up, her face in place.

Her voice was soft and her manners impeccable. She had strong ideas about decorum. She was "a lady," and she struggled mightily to make one of me too.

"Sit up straight, Yvette," she used to say. "Be a lady. Sit still. Don't act like a wild Indian." It was her litany. She said it kindly, but she said it often. Maybe she knew where I came from. Or maybe she'd have worked just as hard with any little girl, smoothing the rough edges, grooming her to be "a little lady."

Memories crowded in, pulling me back to my hometown of Neponsit, which was then a privileged enclave on the Rockaway Peninsula of the borough of Queens, New York. The air was fresh and tangy, scented with sea and salt. The wild surf of the Atlantic Ocean was just a block away. The quieter waters of the bay were a short walk in the other direction. The only sounds were the whoops of children at play on streets where strangers seldom ventured. On-street parking was against the law here, discouraging outsiders, leaving the beach private and the streets safe.

Ours was the big, white clapboard house with the front door painted red. Have I said that Bea's favorite color was red, or any shade thereof? I slept under a pink silk canopy, trimmed with white eyelet, in a room designed for a little princess. "Just like in the movies," my cousin Robin used to say. The view from my window looked over the trees and down a street where I knew everyone's name.

"I built this house just for you, Yvette," Larry Silverman used to tell me. He was forty-seven when I came into his life, a barrel-chested man with dark hair already flecked with gray and moving north. He was a short man, looking even shorter when he stood next to Bea. With little formal education, he was a self-taught, self-made man. There was no device, no appliance, no broken toy that he couldn't fix. Along with his partner, Leonard Levy, he built Leonard's Radio into a prosperous chain of TV and electronics stores. It made him a millionaire at a time when a dollar was a dollar, and having a million of them meant being seriously rich.

"This is your house," he told me. If he said it once, he said it a dozen times. "It will always be Yvette's house." He meant it when he said it. I was sure of that. But life takes unexpected turns, and "always" is a dangerous promise to make.

There were secrets in that big house. "Where did I come from?" I used to ask. But there were things we didn't talk about. "Who is my other mother?" I wanted to know. But Bea and Larry always changed the subject, and I learned not to press it. They were Mom and Dad, and I was firmly attached to them. Back then, I was only mildly curious about the phantom parents who'd given birth to me.

My adoptive parents shared an enduring love affair, the kind you sigh over in old movies and envy in real life. Bea and Larry never fought; they made each other laugh; they were considerate and affectionate. But in many ways, they were an odd couple, very different from one another. And they had very different ideas about the child they were raising as their own.

Bea wanted a little girl in ruffled dresses, a lady-in-the-making, a blond version of herself. She curled my hair and dressed me like a princess. She read books to me and played pretty songs on the piano. She worried over me, as if at any minute I might shatter into a million pieces.

Every night at dinner, she made certain that there was never a knife, not so much as a butter knife, at my place setting. "You might hurt yourself," she'd explain, cutting my meat for me. She did that even as I grew older, even with my age climbing into double digits. I used to roll my eyes. "For heaven's sake," I used to think to myself, "this woman thinks I'm going to sever an artery and bleed to death."

She filled my days with piano lessons, ballet lessons, tap-dancing lessons, and art classes. Her great triumph came when I played at the famed Carnegie Hall in New York City. I was only five, according to the calendar my parents were going by, and it was only a recital of my piano teacher's students. But for my mother, breathless with excitement, it was the glittering debut of a child prodigy.

She glowed and I grumbled. "Do I have to?" I asked. I was buttoned into a black velvet dress trimmed with a white collar and cuffs. On my feet were patent-leather Mary Janes. On my lips was a cold sore that felt as big as a baseball. I longed to be somewhere else, anywhere else. I looked out at an endless sea of red velvet seats. I sat down to play Brahms' Lullaby, and I was certain that everyone's eyes were focused on that cold sore. Did I hit any clinkers? Did anyone notice? When I stood up, curtsied, and skittered off the stage, there was the amazing, thunderous sound of applause.

I couldn't wait to get out of there. "You were brilliant," my mother said. "Just brilliant." But she was my mother. What else would she say? She thought it was "brilliant" when I learned to tie my own shoes.

Still, I believed her. She never lied to me. And her praise had its effect. It was the beginning of my self-confidence. She shuttled me from piano lessons to ballet classes, expecting me to shine. She always insisted on a straight-A report card. She handed me one challenge after another. "You can do it, Yvette," she kept saying. "Of course, you can." She kept pouring on the praise, lavish and unstinting, and I grew sure of myself and sassy. I had more self-confidence than I really deserved, but in the rocky times that lay ahead, I would need every ounce of it.

With Bea, I learned things. With Larry, I did stuff. He wanted a pal, someone to go bike-riding with, someone to initiate into the mysteries of his home workshop and darkroom. He was the one who took me to a nearby park, letting me run until I was breathless. Sometimes, though we never told Bea about it, he helped me climb one of the trees.

One day, he taught me a daring feat: how to hang by my knees from a tree limb. I was eager, and I learned quickly. After a few tries, he no longer had to hold on to me. I could dangle there on my own, upside-down and giddy. "That's it. Now hold it," he told me. "Just hold it." I hung by my knees while he grabbed for his camera; he was documenting my life in black-and-white snapshots. I held my breath while he checked his light meter. I could hear the limb creaking under my weight when, finally, he snapped the picture.

On the way home, my hand swinging in his, he told me a secret. "You know, Yvette," he said, "I really wanted the boy." I gave him a puzzled look, and then he explained which boy he was talking about.

"You have a twin," he told me. "He's a boy who looks just like you."

Somehow, I felt no surprise. The idea of a twin brother seemed oddly familiar, like something I'd always known but, for a time, had forgotten. "So where is he?" I asked. "What's his name? Can he come over to play?"

If Larry knew a name, he didn't tell me. He explained that the boy lived too far away to visit. Where? He shrugged his shoulders.

"When we found you," he explained, "they told us that there were two children, a boy and a girl who were twins. And I really wanted the boy." He bent down to kiss the tip of my nose. "I fell in love with you the minute I saw you. But, before that, I wanted the boy."

It was my turn to shrug my shoulders. I felt no twinges of hurt or rejection. If he wanted a son, I could come very close. I could play the part. In a lot of ways, I was my own missing twin. I was growing up as a twofer, a proper little girl for Bea, a tomboy for Larry.

The real Yvette was always a mystery, hidden behind those changeable masks. Growing up, a veteran of all those music and dance classes, I knew how to perform on cue. Early on, I learned how to play the part that was handed me, to fulfill expectations and to act like whoever it was that someone else wanted me to be.

Years later, when my life turned unpredictable, it was a survival skill. But now, heading west, I was engaged in something more complicated. No more role-playing. I was struggling to figure out who I myself wanted me to be.

As a child, being a tomboy seemed to come naturally to me. Being a lady was always a bit harder. "My beautiful girl," Bea used to say with a smile. If I stole away from piano practice, she always knew where to find me, at the playground, sweaty and shooting hoops with the boys. "My little Indian," she used to sigh.

What did she know? And when did she know it? I needed answers, but I was ashamed of the questions. What did I think I was doing, playing prosecutor with my beloved Mom?

In the view from the rearview mirror, I came to some conclusions. Did she know I was born an Indian? Maybe, but I could live with that. I remembered her warm smile and the way she chanted her litany, over and over. "Sit up straight, Yvette," she was always saying. "Be a lady. Sit still. Don't act like a wild Indian." She believed in the scientific wisdom of her day—in the triumph of nurture over nature—and she meant no harm.

Did she know my true age? Possibly, but I could accept that too. When they were looking for a child, Bea and Larry were turned down by one adoption agency after another. At the time, they were considered "too old" and they had to do something called private adoption. When they were finally offered a child, they may have gone along with a make-believe age. If I walked and talked like an older child, they may have pretended that, as Bea always said, I was "brilliant." If I was taller than most of the other girls in first grade, they pretended not to notice. In one of Larry's photographs, I could be seen towering over a girl cousin who was close to my supposed age. But by destiny, by genes, I never grew past five feet four, and before very long, I was towering over no one.

That still left the big question. Did she know I was stolen? Hungry for a child, did she play any role in that?

I remembered Bea, the caring mother, the Lady Bountiful, always quick to take in strays, always ready to offer her hand, her help, her chicken soup to anyone who needed it. One time, she dragged home an old homeless man whom she'd found on the street. "Poor man," she said. "Doesn't he look like *zaydeh*?" She was talking about her father, the grandfather who had died soon after I was adopted. She put the man to bed in our guest room. She fed and cared for him for more than a week. Then she sent him off in one of Larry's best suits, with some money tucked in a pocket.

That was Bea. The woman who did that was not a thief. She would not have traveled to Florida in her high heels and her silk dress, to pick up a contraband child. Not Bea. She would not have had any part in a plot to steal another woman's child. Later on, if she came to suspect that I was stolen, she would not have rested easy with that thought. In my mind's eye, I could see her marching off in search of the truth. Her only stop might have been the beauty parlor, to have her hair done—and mine.

I felt less certain about Larry. As he once told me, it was Bea who wanted a child, not him. She was desperate to adopt, and he was desperate to please her. As I had seen for myself, there was nothing he wouldn't do to make her happy. "I fell in love with you at first sight," he always told me. But in that first moment, as he hugged and kissed me, he could have known that I was a stolen child. He could have told himself that I'd be better off with him than with "a wild Indian" for a father. He could have convinced himself that it was a good deed in disguise. Maybe, thinking that he'd already done so much for me, that was why he ended up leaving me out of his will.

All those years ago, being adopted was the wallpaper of my life, the background that was always there, something I never thought about changing. Occasionally, though, I was curious. In one of the rooms in our house, the walls were covered with a heavy linen weave, and I used to tug at the threads, pulling them out, unraveling the design. "Where did I come from?" I wondered now and then, pulling at the threads of my life. "Who is my other mother?" I asked from time to time, longing to unravel the design.

Larry was in his darkroom that Saturday afternoon when my friend Marla Karen came over to play. Outside, it was raining hard. We were eight, housebound and restless, poking around the den for something to do. To liven things up, I told her my secret.

"You know what? I have a twin."

Marla rolled her eyes at me. "Sure you do."

I insisted. "It's true. I have a twin brother."

She gave me one of her looks. "No you don't."

I was annoyed. "Yes I do."

Hands on hips, she dared me. "Prove it. Where is he? What does he look like?"

Well, she'd asked the big question, and I didn't have an answer. I needed help. I knocked on the darkroom door until my father emerged.

"Tell her, Dad. Tell her I have a twin." He nodded at Marla, which I took to be a yes. Then he disappeared back into the darkroom. "See, I told you," I crowed to Marla, but she was still making faces at me. A couple of minutes later, Dad was back. He slapped a photograph down on the table.

"Here," he said. "Here's your brother."

It was a black-and-white photograph of a little boy. I stared at the picture. His hair seemed light and I couldn't tell the color of his eyes. Marla examined it closely. "You know, Yvette, he looks like you. He really does." I smiled in triumph. "So where is he?" she asked.

I didn't know. I was tired of trying to prove things to her. "I'm going upstairs now," I told her. "I have to write a letter to my brother."

I did that from time to time, write letters to my/twin brother. Childish letters. "How are you?" I'd write. "I'm fine. I'm in third grade. I like school. Do you? Don't forget to write. Your loving sister, Yvette."

I didn't have a name, much less an address, but I gave the letters to my mother. I assumed she'd address and mail them, just like she addressed and mailed the thank-you notes I wrote for birthday presents. There was never an answer, but I kept writing anyway.

A part of me was missing, but it was distant and dimly remembered. There was the idea of a brother, but not the reality. There were the phantoms of another mother and another father. Sometimes I daydreamed of a royal couple, a king and queen, ceaselessly searching the world for their lost princess. Most of the time, I imagined a young woman with no husband, no money, no way to take care of a baby. I thought how sad she must have been, having to give me away. Sometimes, I wished I could tell her that I was in good hands.

If only she could have known. I was coming home now, but too late to meet her. My birth mother died eight years ago. As the Navajos would say, her spirit returned to the great creator, Father Sun.

She was not the woman I had daydreamed about. She was different from any mother in my wildest imagination.

CHAPTER 3

It was dusk as we moved down the interstate, that in-between hour when the road blurs and it's hard to see clearly. Secrets can break your heart. I blinked at the reflections in my rearview mirror, the twilight shimmer of headlights following behind me, a pair of ghostly eyes above the grimace of grillwork. What you don't know *can* hurt you.

When her twins were stolen, my birth mother lost her balance. "Where are my babies?" she kept asking. She didn't know if we were laughing or crying, healthy or sick, alive or dead, and the not-knowing became a knife in her heart. She had two other children whom she loved, but she was obsessed with the missing ones. Over the years, she would give birth to five more, including another set of twins, but children are not like burned-out lightbulbs, not replaceable, not interchangeable.

For Navajos, the important thing is to find the harmony between all the dualities of this world—Mother Earth and Father Sun, darkness and light, water and fire, body and mind. My mother once had that harmony, but along with her twins, it was stolen from her.

A haunted woman, she slipped deeper and deeper into a black hole of depression, until she could no longer care for her own children. At the same time, work was scarce on the reservation and my father was often absent, laying tracks for the railroad, fixing machinery, traveling as far as California for a desperately needed paycheck.

In hard times, the twins were not the only ones missing from the family circle. All of my brothers and sisters spent some part of their childhoods with a family other than their own. Some of them lived for a time with Navajo relatives; some were raised for a while by a kindly Hopi Indian, a member of the tribe whose reservation is next door to the Navajos'; my sister Darlena even spent a few years with a white family in California.

I heard the story on my first trip to Arizona. "Our mother changed," Darlena told me. "She withdrew from us. She became cold." My youngest sister, Lora, recalled a mother who was "not affectionate." She remembered a woman who was strict about chores. "She woke us up at dawn, and we couldn't go to bed until everything was done. Sometimes, we'd be up past midnight, carding the wool for the rugs our mother used to weave." Yet Lora also remembered something else. "Our mother was always busy, but sometimes she would sit in the chair and I'd see tears running down her face. When I was little, I didn't know about the missing twins, and I didn't understand why my mother was sitting there, crying silently."

A twin like me, born after my disappearance, Lora had no memories of the woman our mother used to be. "We're alike," I told her. "We both missed knowing our real mother."

Betty and Yazzie Monroe never forgot about their lost twins. In family ceremonies, they remembered the missing children in a special prayer. "And sometimes, there were other medicine men who were present," Lora remembered, "and they questioned our parents about it. 'We see two stars, floating in this hogan,' they said, 'and they are like children who are crying. Why are there two children, two stars floating around and crying?' And then Mom and Dad would tell them the story of the missing twins."

The family never stopped looking for the lost children. The search was like a treasured heirloom, passed from mother to daughter and then from sister to sister, until it ended up in the hands of Lora, the kid sister who found me on the Internet. Among the medicine people at Tolani Lake, there were some gifted ones called "Crystal Gazers." People believed that they could gaze into chunks of rock crystal, collected from holy places, and then see across the miles and into the future. Through the years of searching, the Crystal Gazers offered hope to my family. "One day, you will find the twins," they told my parents, over and over. "You will find them where the sun comes up."

My brother was still missing, and it was too soon to know if that prophecy would hold true for him. But I had always been in the east, where the sun comes up, waiting to be found. When it happened, I was in Maine, "Down East," as it's called, as far east as you can go in these United States.

Now, going home, I was moving west. Secrets can be dangerous. I turned around in my seat, craning for a glimpse of Heather's dark head, bent over a book that she was reading in the half light. Not knowing can make you sick. Three years ago, when I had no idea that I might be an Indian, when I had no clue about the genes I had passed on to my daughter, it came close to killing her.

Heather fell desperately ill. Day by day, she grew weaker. Week after week, she lay in bed, pale as the sheets. I wrapped her in blankets and carried her from doctor to doctor, but they couldn't explain why my daughter was wasting away.

As she lost weight, I cooked her favorite foods. "Eat," I begged her, offering some hamburger. "Just one bite," I cajoled, spooning up macaroni and cheese. "Just one sip," I said, holding a glass of milk to her lips. I wanted to stuff her with nutrition but, without knowing it, I was making her even sicker.

The doctors were baffled. They were looking at something they'd never seen before. Unaware of the genes that my daughter and I both carried, I could not give them the clue they needed. Weeks turned into frantic months. Then a specialist in Portland began to rule out one diagnosis after another. Finally, he hit upon the answer, an unusual syndrome that includes a lactose intolerance along with a missing pancreatic enzyme, Lypoprotein Lypase Deficiency, as they called it. The condition is extremely rare among whites, though it's not that uncommon among Indians. As I know now, it runs in my Navajo family.

"Amazing," the doctor said. "You're not Indian, are you?" I shook my head. "Who, me?" As he explained, my daughter's body was rebelling against beef and dairy products, the very foods I'd been trying to feed her. "She needs to eat like an Indian," he told me, prescribing a diet of venison and other wild game.

I searched the stores. Venison was available, prepackaged and beyond our tight budget. I am not ashamed to say that Dickie broke the law, hunting deer out of season to save his daughter's life. Heather made faces at the gamey taste, but the venison revived her. Slowly, her health returned.

Navajos feel a kinship with the animals, and they have a hunter's ritual. If Dickie had known the words, he would have said them to that slain deer: "We thank you for your life. Brother, we know that your life is as precious as ours.

But we also know that one life must sometimes give way to another, so that the one great life of all may continue unbroken." Some Navajos believe that if the bullet or the arrow finds its mark, it is because the animal has agreed to yield up its life; if it misses, it is because the animal has said no.

Dickie shifted in the passenger's seat, trying to find a comfortable position for a back that was riddled with arthritis. Heather and Lori were focused on dinner. "McDonald's," Heather was saying, pleading for her favorite food, fast or not. "Please, Mom. Please, let's stop at the next one." I agreed. With time, she seemed to be outgrowing her near-fatal allergies. I watched her slather on the ketchup. With every hamburger, I still watched her like a nervous Jewish mother, scanning for any sign of a symptom.

Time was a healer. So was knowledge. Heather fell sick because we were ignorant of who she and I were. She regained her lost health at about the same time as we regained our lost past. It might be coincidence. Or it might not. Not knowing who you are can mean being out of synch with yourself. Navajos believe that healing can take place only when there's harmony between body and spirit.

For now, the harmony I was searching for was between my muddled past and my mysterious future. I looked for road markers. Now and then, I caught sight of a sign in a storefront restaurant: "Kosher Deli." Here and there, on the menu of a roadside diner, I spotted bagels and "Jewish-style" rye bread. Fewer and further between, I glimpsed a Star of David carved in stone on a synagogue building. My heart leaped, as it always had, at those familiar signs. "I could go there," I thought. "I could feel at home there."

There were other signs, mixed signals that I'd never paid attention to before. Injun Joe's Cafe blinked in red neon. The ladies' room at one roadside stop was marked "Squaws." We passed Geronimo's Garage and the Wampum thrift shop, but I didn't think Indians owned either of them. No more than they owned the Atlanta Braves.

I was looking for intersections. Some people, for instance, said that the Indians were one of the Lost Tribes of Israel. The two languages seemed to have some words in common, such as *shaman* for an Indian medicine man and *shammes* for a synagogue sexton. When I first heard that, I grasped at the idea. Any straw will do when you're drowning in doubts, but I've since let go of this one.

The idea that the Indians might be a Lost Tribe of Israel originated with the Mormons, who claimed it was part of a divine revelation. Inspired by it, Mormon missionaries flocked to the reservations, eager to convert the Indians for life in the hereafter. They know better now, but some Mormons used to have a saying about Indians: "We'll whiten them, and then we'll delight in them."

Indians have no need to piggyback on someone else's identity. They have a past, a history, a story of their own. They existed long before Columbus "discovered" them. Archaeologists have found traces of Indian civilization in North America that go back as far as 30,000 years. That's long before those Ten Tribes of Israel disappeared into the mist.

"Maybe," one of my Navajo cousins suggested to me, "it's the other way around." He gave me a sly smile. "Maybe the Jews are one of the lost tribes of Indians."

On a makeshift Vision Quest, there are wrong turns and blind alleys, but there are also pathways that lead somewhere. I was looking for the crossroads where my identities might meet.

I clutched at any similarity I could find between the two religions. The Navajo language has no word for religion: it doesn't need to be named; it is something that is just there, always present, woven into the fabric of daily life. They have no concept of heaven or hell; their focus is on living well and honorably in this world. When you die, your spirit returns to the cosmos, no more separate and identifiable than a drop of water that's returned to a lake.

To me, that felt comfortable and familiar. Growing up Jewish, I believed in both a heaven and a hell, but I heard very little talk about either. Judaism is a religion stuffed with rules and regulations but, like the Navajos, most of the laws have to do with how to lead a good, ethical life on this earth. Of all the world's great religions, Judaism may be the one closest to the Navajos. Jews do not talk about a personal relationship with a savior, and neither do Navajos. Instead, both peoples talk about a personal relationship with a community, and both feel a personal obligation for the well-being and survival of their community.

For both peoples, there is a special feeling about land, an eternal bond to a particular place that each says was given to them by God or the Great Creator. For Navajos, it lies at the Four Corners, where four American states meet— Arizona, New Mexico, Utah, and Colorado. It is the stretch of wide Southwest mesas and dry deserts, dotted with red rocks and deep blue canyons, its borders marked by four sacred mountains. Four, as my newfound family has told me, is a sacred number, marking the directions, the borders, the proportions of life.

On my first visit to the reservation, my heart quickened with the meaning and the mystery of that land. I had felt that once before, in Israel. As a child, I ended every Passover seder with a shout: "Next year in Jerusalem!" On the edge of adulthood, I lived in Israel for two years, fighting there in the Yom Kippur War, planning to make it my permanent home. Israel was where I fell in love for the first time. Israel was where I killed a man. Israel . . . But I wasn't ready yet to think about that.

Whoever I was, she was formed back in Neponsit. I had an identity there. I was Bea and Larry's kid. When I stepped out of our red front door, there were lots of other kids to play hide-and-seek with, or cowboys-and-Indians. I was always one of the Indians, because they were supposed to be wilder, which I liked, and they were the underdogs, which I always preferred.

The neighborhood was middle class or better, and most of the families we knew were Jewish, like us. It was cozy and safe, like a private club where everybody is the same. As a child, I never heard an anti-Semitic word.

But some of the neighbors wondered about me. Especially with my hair curled, I looked more like Shirley Temple than Barbra Streisand.

"It's funny," a neighbor told me. "You don't look Jewish."

I scowled at her. "But I am."

"Well, you don't look it."

"I am Jewish," I insisted. "I'm as Jewish as anyone."

Everyone knew I was adopted, but one little boy liked to tease me. "*Goy*," he called me. "Yvette's a *goy*." As I'd been taught, it wasn't polite to call someone names. So I socked him. He pulled my blond hair, and I socked him again.

We were Jews, no doubt about it, but we were not especially devout. We were culinary Jews, gathering on Friday evenings for a traditional feast that began with chicken soup and matzoh balls. Like the grandmothers on the reservation, my Grandma Sophie was the guardian of memory, the keeper of the Jewish flame. She was Bea's mother, always there, always filling my head with legends of Jewish heros, with stories of long-ago weddings where she'd danced the *horah*, and with tales of life in the Old Country. Sometimes, sitting at our table, she'd start to cry, remembering an uncle or a cousin who had stayed behind in Poland and had perished in the Holocaust.

Our little neighborhood had five synagogues, but as a

family, we were not regulars at any of them. We went to synagogue for bar mitzvahs and for the big events, for the High Holy Days of Rosh Hashanah and Yom Kippur. My father was there because he believed in it. My mother was there "for the sake of the relatives," because her absence might offend one of them. As for me, I was there to solve the mystery of the ark.

The ark, looking like a deep closet of heavily carved wood, stood on the eastern wall of the synagogue, facing toward Jerusalem. They kept the Torah scrolls in that ark, but what else was hidden in the shadows? It looked deep enough for a little girl to hide in. If she did, would God speak to her? Or would he smite her?

I thought about it a lot. My friend Marla Karen and I whispered about it. We made plans to come back to the synagogue after everyone else had left and explore the ark. We prided ourselves on being bold little girls. We double-dared each other. But this was solemn and scary. After the service, there was the kiddish ceremony, with wine for the grownups and tables loaded with sponge cake and macaroons. And Marla and I allowed ourselves to be distracted.

Although we were Jewish, Bea was also something else—a Christian Scientist. She'd turned to that religion because of an illness that began before I was adopted. That illness was one of the secrets in our house, seldom talked about, never named. I know now that it was Bright's Disease, a painful, often life-threatening disorder of the kidneys. Doctors now have another, jawbreaking name for it: chronic glomerulonephritis.

Bea was a vibrant woman, active and tireless, when I came into her life. She had years of remission, and she credited Christian Science for that. "Sickness is an error," she used to tell me. It was a mistake, a distortion, a sign of a lack of faith. If her faith was strong enough, she believed, then her body would heal itself. "God promises," she told me.

Across the years, her words were a long-ago echo of what I was now hearing from my Navajo family. They too believed that sickness was a distortion, a signal that the person was out of harmony with the universe. Unlike Bea, they didn't spurn modern medicines or avoid doctors. But when those doctors were baffled by an illness, they turned to the ancient ways. They believed that the patient wouldn't be cured until you removed the underlying cause of the illness, the disharmony. The Navajos may be the world's first psychosomatic practitioners. Or the oldest New Agers. They believed that if you wanted to heal the body, you must also treat the spirit.

Harmony—it was at the core of Navajo belief, and it was part of Bea's religion too. Striving to achieve it, she spent long hours reading, praying, and attending Christian Science services. But when I was going on ten, at least according to the calendar my parents were following, she began to weaken and lose the struggle.

Looking back, I remembered the day it began.

I was all set to go, my tutu and ballet slippers in the bag, ready to leave for my dance lesson. When I went looking for Bea, I found her in her room, asleep on the bed, lying there fully dressed, just her shoes off, looking strangely vulnerable. That was a first; she'd never forgotten a dance lesson. That was odd; Bea was full of energy, not the kind of woman to be caught napping during the day. I didn't wake her. Instead, happy to have a free afternoon, I tiptoed down the stairs and then ran outside to find my playmates.

The signs were obvious, but I was a child, oblivious and slow to catch on. A few days later, she was seated in an armchair, staring out the window, a book open on her lap. "Yvette," she asked, "help me." She needed a hand to get out of the chair. She wanted an arm to lean on as she walked up the stairs. A week later, she napped through another dance lesson. The following week, she also missed her usual Wednesday night meeting at the Christian Science church, and that did make me uneasy. Bea missing one of those meetings was about as common as a solar eclipse.

Little by little, she was slowing down. As the weeks passed, she forgot more of my music and dance lessons. The weeks turned to months, and then the stairs to her top-floor bedroom became too much for her. She moved into my room, "for a little while," she said. I moved next door to the guest room, the one with the woven wall covering, the one whose threads I could pick and pull at.

"Don't worry, Yvie," she told me. "I'm a little weak, but I'll be fine soon." As a Christian Scientist, she could not say that she was "sick." Instead, she spent more time than ever at her readings and her prayers.

The piano teacher still came to the house twice a week, but the drives to dancing classes were over. Life was beginning to change, but I tried not to worry. Larry seemed anxious and distracted, but if Bea promised that she'd be fine soon, I had to believe her. There were axioms in geometry and truisms in our house. One was that Bea always kept her promises.

Meanwhile, I was giddy with my new freedom. I didn't expect it to last very long, and I wanted to take advantage of the hours that now stretched before me, uncluttered by dance classes. My friends and I formed a Nature Lovers Club, and I scoured the beach for show-and-tell specimens— bits of blue-green sea glass, interesting shells, or, the best trophy of all, the smelly carcass of a sand shark.

When I was eleven, I organized my friends into another club to hold seances. Marla Karen and Jamie Kushnik were members, along with three or four boys. We met in a little room off my garage, and I was the chief swami.

"I call on the spirits from the north and from the south,"

I said. We sat in a circle, huddled together in that small dark room, with just a single flickering candle to help us see the Ouija board. "I call on the spirits from the east and from the west." We held hands, listening for an answer. "Is anyone there?" We asked for a response. "Give us a sign." We heard one knock, then two.

"Stop it, Billy," I said. "Cut it out." But he insisted it wasn't him.

"Speak to us," I said. We called on the spirits of dead people we knew, like my grandfather, and famous people we didn't know, like Houdini. We tried to talk to them through the Ouija board. "Can you hear us?" Everyone's hands were on the pointer, with mine giving it a little nudge to spell out y-e-s.

I didn't believe that the dead would speak to us, not really. The aim of the game was to scare Marla, which we usually did. But then the air moved. I felt a light wind. Was it just the drafty garage? Or was it a spirit from the great beyond? Sometimes, in the darkness, I also scared myself.

Back in the house, I found Mom sitting in an armchair, looking pale, listening to music on the stereo. She no longer had the energy to play the piano. She smiled at me. "I'll be better soon, Yvie," she said. "God promises."

She was spending more and more time in bed. As I came and went, I always stopped to look in on her. Usually, the room was dark, to help her rest. If the light was on, she was reading and praying. "I'm getting better, Yvette," she told me. "I can feel it." Sometimes she'd come downstairs to read. Sometimes she'd sit in the garden, but she'd tire after just half an hour.

Her main practitioner, Ben Rippie, often came to the house to pray with her. "I don't understand," I heard her tell him one time. "I'm not getting any better." He told her to be strong, to have faith, to keep praying. He suggested that she focus on different readings and different sections of the Bible, like the parable of the mustard seed. "Trust in God," he advised her, "and he will heal you."

Larry, though, was growing frantic. "Let me call a doctor," he pleaded with her. "What harm could it do?" But Bea refused. As time passed, he begged her again. "Please, Bea darling, let me call a doctor. Do it for my sake." But she was adamant.

He was spending more and more time at his business. At home, he was usually in his darkroom. I still joined him in there, but he was somber now and unresponsive. I rattled on about school. I told him about a race I'd won for the track team. But he was preoccupied and didn't seem to be listening. The darkroom was no longer fun, and I went there less and less.

For my twelfth birthday, Larry and Maria, our live-in maid, carried Bea downstairs, her arms around their two shoulders, her feet never touching the ground. She was a shrinking woman in a silk dress, a shadow of herself. There were gifts and a cake with candles. She stayed for almost an hour and then, exhausted, she was carried back upstairs. It was one of the last times she left her bed.

As my life changed, I looked in the mirror and saw a stranger. The *shayneh maydele* was gone. Bea was no longer there to pin up my hair in curls and to slip ruffled dresses over my head. I was in jeans now, like all the other girls, and there were budding new breasts under my tee-shirt. Even my hair was unfamiliar, a change that began with the onset of Bea's illness. At age twelve, it was dark brown and hung long and stringy. I stared at myself in the mirror. I wanted my old life back. I wanted my blond hair back.

With two girlfriends, I went shopping for hair dye. I chose blond for myself and so did one of my friends. The other one chose a shade of red. We brought the hair-dye kits back to my bathroom. We tried to follow the instructions, dabbing on the thick liquid, timing it carefully, gasping at the ammonia fumes that came from all three of our heads. When we were done, washed, rinsed and dried, two blondes and one redhead admired themselves in the mirror.

That evening, an angry mother rang our bell. Larry answered the door and had his first encounter with another parent. She wanted to know how her brown-haired daughter had been turned into a redhead. She blamed me, probably rightly, because I was the ringleader.

"Yvette," my adoptive father demanded, "what's wrong with you?" He was flustered; Bea had always been the one to handle these situations. "How could you let that girl do that?" He apologized to the woman, promising to deal with me.

Looking right at me, he didn't say a word about my own new-old hair color. He didn't seem to notice that I too had changed. I understood. I didn't blame him. He didn't seem to notice very much about me in those days.

It was becoming scary to look at my mother. Still losing weight, she was swollen now. No one named her illness, no one talked about her disease, but her kidneys were shutting down. She became swollen and puffy, lying there like an inflated doll. Her skin was stained with brown spots and scattered with oozing sores. Was she in pain? She had to be, but she never said so and never complained. "God promises," she kept telling me. "I'll be better soon."

I was going on thirteen, a girl in a hurry. "Don't walk," was my motto. "Run!" I was racing out of my room and down the hallway when I saw my mother, sitting at the top of the stairs. By that time, she rarely got out of bed, and I didn't know why she was there, but Maria was coming up the stairs toward her.

Did my loose shirt, flying behind me, brush against my mother? Suddenly, she screamed. "You hit me! Why did you hit me?" Clinging to the stair rail, she was crying in pain and wailing. "My own child hit me. My own child hurt me."

My mind reeled. I was confused and frightened. "I didn't hit you," I started to say. But my adoptive mother, once so calm and beautiful, was shaking and hysterical. Maria helped her back to bed, calming her down, staying at her side until she fell asleep.

I went downstairs and wept at the kitchen table. "I didn't hit her," I kept thinking. "I didn't touch her." But I remembered that shirt, flying loose, brushing against her skin, swollen and painful with sores. Carelessly, without meaning to, I had hurt her.

Eventually, I stopped crying. But I never stopped feeling guilty.

The end came on a Saturday morning, my time to be in art school. My father sat by my mother's bed, watching as she drifted in and out of consciousness. She was like a caricature of herself, her proud body swollen with disease, her skin tormented by cruel itching, her limbs twitching in sudden spasms of pain. A faint smell, like rotting fruit, rose from a wasted body that weighed less than ninety pounds. My father sat there for a long time, weeping. And then he called for an ambulance.

Some sixth sense woke my mother. She heard him on the phone. "No, Larry, no," she pleaded. "No, Larry, don't do it." She had endured for years, trusting in the promises of Christian Science. To the very end, she clung fiercely to that faith. "Please, Larry," she begged. But my father was as desperate as she was. His wife was dying, and he could no longer sit there, doing nothing.

When I came home, Maria told me what had happened.

Sirens screaming, the ambulance arrived. My mother heard and wept. The paramedics took one look at my mother and started an intravenous solution. My mother pushed them away. They tried to hold her down, but she felt the IV needle going in. Weak as she was, my mother pulled it out. They tried to give her a sedative, but she clamped her mouth shut.

Light as a child, she was placed on a stretcher. "Help me, Larry," she gasped. My father bent to kiss her, but his mind was made up. All he wanted to do was keep her alive. Against her will, she was taken to the hospital.

The next day was Sunday, November 26, 1967. I was taken to visit her in the hospital. She lay on the bed, white as the sheets, insubstantial as a ghost. I felt shaken and terrified, but I wouldn't let myself cry. She looked half dead, but she had told me she would get better. And I held tightly to that promise.

All around her bed, IV bottles hung on their stands, unused. A nurse told me that she had managed to insert a needle, but my mother had ripped it out. She tried again, and Bea ripped it out again. They had tried to give her pills for her pain, but each time, she would spit them out. No one understood where she got the strength. She shouldn't have been able to lift a feather, but she still fought off the nurses and doctors.

I have read about my adoptive mother's disease. Early on, doctors might have had a chance to stop its progress with special drugs, diet, and diuretics. Later, they might have tried to save her with dialysis or even a transplant. At this point, all they could do was try to make her more comfortable, and she would not allow even that. They stepped back, respecting her wishes, amazed that she had lasted this long. With her disease in its advanced stages, she had lived longer than any doctor would have predicted. Her faith kept her from medical help, but maybe it was also what gave her those extra years.

That day in the hospital, I barely recognized my mother, and she didn't seem to know that I was there. She had slipped into a coma, but her arms and legs were thrashing under the thin sheet.

"You'll have to leave now," a nurse told me. Hands on my shoulders, leading me out, she explained that children weren't really allowed in the hospital.

My father was outside in the hallway, his face ashen, his eyes red. "Come with me, Yvette," he said. He led me out of the hospital and down the street. We walked for a while, until we came to a movie theater. *Bonnie and Clyde* was playing. My father bought a ticket for me and led me inside. He talked to the woman who was standing by the door, serving as the ticket-taker and usher. "I want you to wait here for a while," he told me. "Just find a seat and stay there. The woman will keep an eye on you."

I'd never been in a movie theater by myself before. It was midafternoon and mostly empty. I found a seat and tried to focus on the screen. The picture had already started, and I couldn't quite tell what the actors were up to. I don't know how long I looked at that movie when something strange, something I still can't explain, started to happen.

The screen began to blur. It flickered and went dim. I couldn't see the actors anymore and I couldn't hear their voices. I felt calm and unafraid. In that moment, I sensed my mother's presence and I heard her voice.

"I have to go now," she was saying. "I love you, but I have to say good-bye." Even as I listened to her words, I wondered if I was imagining it. My mother was in the hospital, but her familiar voice was in my ears.

"I don't want to go, but it's time," she was telling me. "I love you more than anything. I told Daddy to take care of you. I told him that you should always come first." As if in a dream, my mother was reaching out to speak to me. "I don't want to leave you, but I have to. Good-bye, my darling. Don't be afraid."

Then she was gone. In my mind's eye, I had a vision of

my father coming down the aisle. The usher was guiding him with her flashlight. "That poor child," she was saying. "Oh, that poor child."

Then the screen brightened. I could see the actors again. I could hear their voices again. But, just as in my dream, I could also hear footsteps coming down the aisle. The usher was coming closer with her flashlight. Wide awake now, I stared straight ahead. "If I turn around," I thought, "it won't be a dream. It will be real." I heard the usher saying, "Oh, that poor child." I put my hands over my ears. "No, I don't want this," I thought. "No, it can't be real."

But my father was at my side, taking my hand. "I know," I said to him. "Mommy is gone."

Grandma Sophie was waiting outside the movie theater. My Uncle Herbie was there, and my Aunt Ceil. My father's station wagon was parked at the curb. I blinked in the light of the real world. My father's eyes were red from crying, and his face was gray. In the two hours or so since he'd left me at the movies, he had aged ten years.

"Mommy came to talk to me," I told him. Standing there on the sidewalk, I thought he'd want to know what she said. "She told me that she didn't want to leave me, but she had to." At that moment, my mother's death was still unreal. I didn't believe that she was gone, but I did believe that I had heard her voice. And I wanted to tell my father what she'd said. "She told me that she loved me more than anything. She said that I should always come first."

My father took a step back. "How do you know that? Who told you?" he demanded. "Who was here before me?" He seemed very angry.

"No one told me," I said. "Only Mommy was here."

My father's face was twisted. It was a mask of grief and fury. He lifted his hand and then, swinging hard, he slapped my face.

"Liar!" he said.

I turned to stone. I couldn't move. I couldn't speak. I could hardly breathe. My face stung and turned red with the mark of his hand. He'd never slapped me before. He'd never called me names before. But he was a practical man, frightened at what he couldn't touch, confused and angry at what he couldn't understand, haunted by what he had lost.

Everyone got in the station wagon. Grandma Sophie sat next to me, and I clung to her, too frightened to cry. She too didn't understand. "How did you know, Yvette?" she asked. "How could you know?"

At the end, as my grandmother told me, my mother was unconscious, but she was talking. She seemed to think that I was in the room with her, and she was talking to me. The words I heard in the movie theater were my mother's last words, spoken in the hospital before she died.

Steering west now, covering the miles between an old life and a new one, I remembered my mother's words, and my father's. In that moment on the sidewalk, standing outside the movie theater, everything changed between Larry and me. He began to keep his distance from me.

Just when we needed each other the most, we mourned separately. We passed each other in the hallways, barely speaking, more like strangers than father and daughter.

I too was angry. I was angry at Bea, who had broken her promise, betraying me by dying. I was angry at Christian Science, for not keeping its own promises to Bea, for somehow letting her down. I was a child, and I was even angry at God, for taking away the only mother I'd ever known.

Bea was gone, and we were no longer a family. Bea was gone, and so was all harmony from that big white house in Neponsit.

CHAPTER 4

"A re we there yet?"

My daughter Lori was impatient. We were moving through the flat stretches of New Mexico, a lone car on an empty road that wound past the buttes and mesas. I had to adapt to a strange, new landscape. I had to adjust my eyes. Maine had been rolling hills and towering mountains, green in summer, covered in white snow in winter, scented always with the salty smell of a crashing sea. This was different, endless and empty, shifting shades of beige and brown that could turn blue in a shadow or be struck by the sun and turn gold or orange-red or even Georgia O'Keeffe pink. With nothing to break the view, the sky went on forever.

"Are we there yet?"

Weary of driving across country, I was impatient too. And so was Dickie. The trip was longer and harder than we'd expected, and he was not doing well. He was coughing his way across the country, struggling with a cold, maybe something worse, maybe the emphysema that was acting up. He had ruined his health in a lifetime of hard smoking, hard drinking, and hard physical work as a farmer, a fisherman, a carpenter. Along the way, he'd broken a number of bones, not all of them set well, some of them making him grit his teeth now against the pain.

"Almost," I said. "We're almost there."

We cheered as we passed the landmark sign: "You are now entering the Navajo Reservation." We crossed the border into a special place, a nation within a nation. It was winter, the Time When Thunder Sleeps. The tourists were gone, and so were the roadside souvenir stands. They'd be back in spring, selling their turquoise necklaces and silver concha belts, their hand-thrown pottery and hand-woven rugs, some of it authentic, some of it not so real.

Soon, we spotted our first hogan, the traditional hut made of logs and covered with mud and twigs. On its round roof was another sign of the times, a satellite TV dish. I had to smile. Before long, there were other hogans, sometimes three or four in a row, most of them with dishes set on the roof or in the yard, pointing to the sky.

Cultures meet. Cultures merge. I've been told that it's the Navajo way. The *Dineh* got corn and weaving from the Hopis, horses and sheep from the Spaniards, satellite dishes and pickup trucks from the *belagaana*, the white Americans. The trick was to figure out what new things you wanted to take and what old ways you wanted to keep.

After all the miles, my Vision Quest was limping along in stops and starts, incomplete but ecumenical. Each night, I fell exhausted into a motel bed. In my last waking moment, I did what I've always done. I murmured the *Shema*, the Hebrew prayer. *Shema Yisroel, Adonai elohaynu, Adonai echod.* Hear O Israel, the Lord our God, the Lord is One.

And then, in my own way, I talked to God. "C'mon

God," I said. "I need some help here. Get us there faster.
Get us there in one piece."

We had one more day to go, and what then? Dickie
went for hours without speaking, and not just because of
his aches and pains. I knew what he was thinking about. I
understood what was troubling him. I never should have
told him what my sisters had said about him.

"A white man?" one sister asked when she heard about
my husband. "It makes my skin crawl," she said, "to think
of laying down with a white man."

In mid-sentence, as I repeated the words, I knew how
they would hurt Dickie. But I've never liked keeping secrets,
and it just slipped out. It had hurt me too, when I first heard
it. I could feel the hot blood rushing to my face, and angry
words to my lips. Dickie had always been my protector,
leaping in at any hint of a slur against me, but now he was
the one who needed defending.

Dickie was pulling up roots that ran deep in Maine;
Melansons had lived there for generations. He was leaving
his own family behind, so that I could live with mine. But
what kind of welcome was I taking him to? I could feel the
familiar twinge of guilt. I could feel the doubts about this
cross-country move come surging back.

"He's your husband, and we accept him," my sister had
added quickly. She sounded sincere, but this was my first
hint of the anti-white undercurrents that ran through Tolani Lake.

"White people are treacherous," another sister said.
"You can't trust them." I started to interrupt, but she did not
want to hear any lectures from me about tolerance. "C'mon,
Yvette," she said. "Just remember what they did to our
mother. Just think what they did to you."

Prejudice runs deep, and it runs both ways. My Navajo
sisters and brothers grew up hearing stories about white
people who massacred Indians, stole their land, and kid-

napped their children. The old wounds were still unhealed, and there were fresh insults that came with a sharp sting. When my clan relatives went shopping in the border towns of Flagstaff and Winslow, they learned to stick to the few stores that had a reputation as being "Indian-friendly." They told endless stories of sitting in a restaurant, being ignored or treated rudely, waiting forever to be served.

My sisters and brothers came of age distrusting the glass beads and shiny trinkets of the white culture on the one hand, longing for its comforts and technologies on the other. They were still trying to find the harmony between the white world and the red. Each did it in his own way. My brother Pete, a soldier in the United States Army for twenty years, was now a tribal policeman, handsome in his uniform, roaming the reservation in a fully equipped radio car, then coming home to tell his children stories of the old days and the old ways. My bachelor brother Robert, the youngest son, the one who teased the aunties and made them laugh, moved back and forth between the two worlds, disappearing for months at a time, then turning up in Levi's and Nikes, with his dark hair still long, falling halfway down his back, like a Navajo flag of honor.

For our part, Dickie and I were hauling our own baggage, a clutter of stereotypes that we'd picked up from the pop culture, a confusion of images. The Last of the Mohicans. The craggy face on the buffalo nickle. Geronimo on the warpath. The painted faces and half-naked bodies, swooping down on innocent wagon trains. The fearless Mohawks who walked the high steel to build New York's skyscrapers. The nobler-than-thou Indians of *Dances with Wolves*. Who were these people? Wild savages, as Bea used to say, or noble ones? I'd grown up thinking they were extinct, but now I was heading west to live with the all-too-human beings who said they were my family.

Dickie had his own ideas. Like so many Americans, he

was in love with the legendary Indians who no longer existed. He saw them as half-naked Adams who wandered an unspoiled paradise. Even before he knew he'd married an Indian, he longed to be one of them. He used to talk to me about living a hundred or so years ago. Back then, he was sure he'd have been an Indian, galloping across the plains, loin-skin flapping, long hair streaming in the wind. "I was born too late," he used to complain.

Now he worried that they might reject him. Every Navajo we'd met so far had been polite to his face, but what were they thinking about this lean, sunburnt white man? "Go slow," he was told, but that was not Dickie's usual speed. "Give it time," he was advised. "Don't speak too quickly. Learn to listen instead." On both sides, we were going to have to learn to see past the color of the skin to the color of the soul.

And what about me? I was a Jew who belonged to the Navajo Nation and, within it, to my mother's clan and to my father's. I was Tobacco Clan, born for Salt Clan. *Tachii'nii*, born for *Ashiihi*. Or so they told me.

On my visit to Tolani, my brother Pete, a serious man, pointed to a distant mountain where our ancestors once lived. "It's where the wild tobacco grows," he said. "It's where our mother's clan got its name." As he explained, a clan's name usually describes its place of origin, and so, long ago, our father's people, the Salt Clan, must haved lived close to a source for that vital ingredient. Today, members of both clans are scattered across the reservation, and some live outside it. "It doesn't matter where they live," Pete told me. "Each one is your brother or your sister. If you need help, they will give it. If you need shelter, they will take you in."

Would they? I wanted to believe in the promise of those blood ties, but I was afraid to trust too much, too soon.

As I knew, my green eyes were a puzzle. My once-blond

hair was a problem. On that first visit to the rez, Indian shorthand for the reservation, I showed pictures of myself as a child, and people shook their heads. Little Indian girls do not have green eyes. They do not normally have blond hair. Maybe it was an aberration of the genes. Blonde Indians were very rare, but not totally unheard of. "I've seen one blond Indian before. Maybe two," my sister Lora said loyally. "Me too," said another sister, Katie.

Maybe it was the magic of chemistry. As a little girl in Neponsit, I spent long hours at the beauty parlor, having my hair permed and curled. Distrustful of white people, my sisters suspected that, long before my friends and I bought Clairol kits as a preadolescent prank, someone else was bleaching my hair. "Maybe Bea and Larry wanted a blond child," Lora suggested. "Or they wanted to hide who you were." Maybe. But in the first snapshot that Larry ever took of me, just hours after I came to the Silvermans, my hair was already blond.

There was another possibility. And on the rez, it had started people's tongues wagging. "She could be her mother's daughter," some of them were saying, "but maybe not her father's."

That was an old whisper. When the twins went missing, some people speculated that they weren't stolen, as their parents said, but given away because of it. They gossiped about a mysterious, unnamed white man, maybe a seducer, maybe a rapist. In the family, it was a taboo subject. But when my sister Lora inherited the search, she just had to have an answer. As Lora told me, she thought about it for a long time and then, screwing up her courage, she dared to ask our father about it.

"No, no," he told her. His voice was loud and impatient; his face was dark with anger. "They were my children, both of them, the boy and the girl." He remembered that the boy had been born with dark skin, but the little girl was very pale, very light. "They were mine," he repeated, insisting that the children were not given up willingly. When they went missing, he had searched for them and, as he reminded my sister, the family had never stopped trying to find them.

Then my father withdrew into himself. "I do not want to speak on this anymore," he told her.

My original birth certificate was still missing, and no hospital records have been found for me. But there were records from the Winslow Indian Sanatorium for my brother, with a notation that he was a twin. One of those documents had spaces on it for "tribe" and for "degree of blood." In those spaces, forty-three years ago, a hospital official had written "Navajo" and then "4/4," meaning full-blooded. It was only one piece in my identity puzzle, but if that was true of my twin brother, it had to be true of me too.

In the rearview mirror, I caught a glimpse of Lori, my blond child, the daughter who looked most like me. On our first visit to the rez, she was the object of stares, a lone golden head among a gaggle of dark-haired cousins. She would never be just like them, and I would never be just like my sisters.

We grew up hearing different stories, and that shaped us in very different ways. We had lived opposite lives, my sisters and I, and it changed what we saw, even when we were looking at the very same thing. Getting to know one another, my sister Lora and I took long walks around the rez. I heard a great silence, but Lora heard voices from the past. I saw vast stretches of parched earth, but for Lora, the landscape was alive and crowded with memories.

The Navajos tended not to live in villages, clustered together like their Pueblo neighbors, but in hogans and houses that were scattered here and there. Everywhere Lora looked, she saw landmarks, and she pointed them out to me. Behind that desert dune was where the family once lived. Over there, in the other direction, was where her husband Sam came from. "When I was still a child, I was aware of him," she told me, smiling shyly. "I used to see him coming over that ridge, galloping on horseback, and I knew he was for me."

I saw empty spaces, stretches of barren desert that were painted with orange and gold by a setting sun. But she saw the scenes of her childhood. To the right was where she used to visit this aunt and that playmate. To the left was where a ceremonial hogan used to stand.

"And right here, just under our feet," she said, "the grass was green. I used to come here after school to herd sheep for our mother." I looked down at bone-dry sand where it seemed impossible that anything ever grew. "The drought came," she explained, "and then there was no more grass."

I looked at her. I knew what Indians were supposed to do when there was no rain. I'd seen it in those old John Wayne Westerns. "So what about the medicine men?" I asked. "Didn't they do the rain dance?"

Lora laughed. "Yes, sometimes they did. And there was a little rain. But not enough." As she told me, the Navajos did not see the long drought in the same way as the white men did. They did not challenge nature or try to interfere with it. Their task was to be stewards of the land and caretakers of the animals, the birds, even the snakes who lived on it. They did not think about building dams or changing the course of ancient rivers or moving on to a greener place. Instead, they looked for ways to live in harmony with the reality of the world as it was.

The land of the Navajos stretched for 17.5 million acres, or 25,000 square miles, making up one-third of all Indian lands in the lower forty-eight states. Twelve American states have less area than the Navajo country, and the land was bigger than five of those states put together—Connecticut,

Delaware, Maryland, Massachusetts, and Rhode Island. But much of it was leftover land, barren and unwanted by anyone else. Some of it had a breathtaking beauty, and tourists wanted to visit places like the Grand Canyon and the Painted Desert, but not live there, not year in and year out.

The section my family lived on, Tolani Lake, was a small settlement of a few hundred people, with another few hundred living in the surrounding dunes and mesas. But the lake itself was long gone, just a dimly remembered legend. A year earlier, a tourist had driven through, pulling a motor boat. He'd picked the name off a map, hoping for good fishing. When he asked for directions to the lake, people laughed and shook their heads. "If you want to fish on Tolani Lake," they told him, "you better be a time traveler."

For that moment, I was the visitor. I didn't know then if I'd be coming back. I wasn't sure yet about this strange land. Did I belong here? I had lived in so many places, but none had ever felt like this—like home. I seemed to fit right in. I talked with people I'd just met, strangers who called me "daughter" and "sister," and it seemed as if I'd known them all my life. But it was happening too fast, and I found it hard to trust these new feelings.

Ghosts roamed this land. Some of them called to me. Some of them scared me. And what about Dickie, who didn't believe in ghosts? Did he belong here? Did our daughters?

There had been a welcome-home celebration at Chimney Rock, the capital of the Navajo Nation, with then–President Albert Hale there to greet the Lost Bird. There had been a feast at the old family ranch, with plentiful food and abundant gesturing. My father spoke little English and my daughters and I knew no Navajo. But Heather and Lori had fallen in love with my father at first sight; they sat on either side of him, nestling against his broad shoulders, unwilling to let anyone else, even me, sit next to him.

In the evening quiet, Lora and I walked in the empty, trackless middle of nowhere. She was pointing now to another invisible landmark. "Over there, Yvette," she said. "That's where I ran to, on the day I became a woman."

She began to tell me about the coming of age ceremony for girls, and I listened carefully. My own daughters, Lori and Heather, were ten and eleven, racing toward puberty. If we made this our home, this would be their ceremony.

It was called the *kinaalda,* and it was as old as history. Navajos believed that the first one was held for Changing Woman, the mother of us all. It begins as soon as possible after a girl's first menstruation, and it lasts for four days.

On the first day, the girl mixes blue cornmeal, salt, and water into as large a cake as possible. "Mine was three feet in diameter," Lora told me. "It had to feed everyone who was coming to the ceremony. I baked it in an outdoor pit."

By then, our family had built a simple wood-frame house next to the old hogan, but it was in the hogan that all ceremonies took place. At sundown, Lora was washed and dressed in her best velveteen outfit. With it, she wore a silver concha belt and her best turquoise necklaces. She reclined on pillows of cedar boughs, covered with the family's best woven blankets. She faced east, toward the door, toward the rising place of the sacred sun.

It was dark inside the hogan; it was 1973, but electricity had not yet come to Tolani Lake. Shadows, cast by a wood fire, played on the walls. Lora listened carefully as our mother and our aunts talked to her about the pleasures and the responsibilities of being a woman. "They told me that one day I would have to take care of my husband," she remembered, "and I would have to be strong for my children. They would depend on me. I would have to be wise without electricity, as they said. That meant never mind about electricity, never mind about technology. What was important was to have an understanding of life and to have the old knowledge of what it is to be a good human being."

Outside, our father and the other men sat around a campfire, singing through the night. At the first glimmer of light in the east, they were up and shouting, "It's time! Hurry, it's time!" The day was dawning, and so was Lora's life as a woman. She stepped outside, turning from one direction to another, honoring the Holy Women who represent the poles of the four directions—Earth Woman on the east, Mountain Woman on the south, Water Woman on the west, and Corn Woman on the north. She murmured a brief prayer for strength in each direction.

Then Lora began to run toward the east, as far and as fast as she could. The farther she ran, the longer her life would be. The faster she ran, the stronger she would be as a woman. "I ran two miles to this point," she remembered with pride, "and two miles back." When she returned, the family and the guests were cheering. "Ai! You ran well," our father told her. "Your Road of Life will be long and happy!"

Tired but pleased with herself, Lora lay back on her pillows. Our mother, our older sisters and the aunts smoothed her hair; they massaged her body, rubbing, pommeling, and kneading it into the shape of the woman she was to become; they stretched her arms and legs to give her strength and endurance for the challenges of life. Then the corn cake was brought forth, and Lora gave pieces of it to everyone.

For four days, the ceremony was repeated. At each dawn, Lora ran in a different direction. Years before, young men used to hide themselves along the girl's path, jumping out to encourage and then pursue her. "We don't do that anymore," Lora told me, "but they did it in our mother's time. These days, a couple of friends run along with the girl, to keep her company and give her strength. But they have to be careful not to outrun her. Because if she doesn't come in first, she won't have a long life."

On the fourth morning, Lora distributed the last of the corn cake. "Something inside me was changed by that ceremony," Lora remembered. "I had passed a test. I had crossed the line from child to woman. I think I even looked different."

Far away in Neponsit, no one celebrated my own coming of age. No one cheered.

Some of my friends had bat mitzvahs, the Jewish ceremony for girls which occurs on their twelfth or thirteenth birthday. This celebration marks their passage from being a girl to becoming a woman, their path of transformation from being a child to joining the congregation of grownups and participating in all the prayers and rituals. I watched as my friends were called to the front of the synagogue. I listened as they read to the congregation from the Torah, and I saw the proud smiles of my friends' parents. I feasted and danced the *horah* at their parties. But my own thirteenth birthday came and went, and there was no applause and no dancing. No one even seemed to notice.

On the day of Bea's funeral, a sad song was coming from the TV. I turned the volume down low, not wanting Larry, distraught and grieving, to overhear the lament. It was a popular song, "Honey," a simple song about a woman who had died.

"And Honey I miss you . . ." the refrain went. The words went round and round in my head.

"And Mommy I miss you . . ." I thought.

"And Daddy I miss you too . . ."

Bea was gone and Larry was keeping his distance. Once I had been his darkroom pal, his bike-riding buddy, his substitute son. Now, ever since that moment on the sidewalk, standing outside the movie theater, I was something else—

"a liar." One day, desperate to break the silence between us, I discovered that I was something even worse than that.

"Please, Daddy," I began. "Please talk to me." I was close to begging. "Mommy said that you were supposed to take care of me. Mommy said . . ."

He turned to face me. He held up one hand, like a stop sign. "It's your fault," he said, his voice rasping and unforgiving. "You killed her," he told me, and the room began to spin. "If it weren't for you, she'd still be alive."

I remember holding tight to a chair, to keep from falling. I couldn't speak. All I could do was nod my head. Grief had turned my father cold and hard, but he was right. In my heart, I agreed with him. I'd done something terrible to hurt my mother, even if I didn't know what it was. Maybe raising a child like me, sassy and stubborn, had been too much for her. Maybe it was the day I brushed against her. Maybe . . .

Guilt was now my middle name. Long ago, when I was just three years old, two strangers had come to carry me away from another mother figure, that pretty, crying woman. Back then, I knew it was because I must have done something really bad. Now I was fourteen, and I knew it again.

A year after Bea's death, Larry married again. His new wife was Bea's opposite—a woman who was petite and doll-like, her hair salon-stiff and bottle-blond, her blue eyes looking huge and startled behind the strong lenses of her designer glasses. Along with a new mother, I was getting a sister, three years older than me, and a brother, six years older.

For a brief moment, I had the wild idea that we could be a family again. I smiled at my new stepmother and began to call her "Mom," but she put a quick stop to that. "Don't you call me that," she ordered. "For you, my name is Blanche. Or Mrs. Silverman."

My teenage years were like a video of the Cinderella

story, but I was living it on fast rewind. I was unwanted, uninvited to the ball, no fairy godmother in sight. My old room, fit for a princess, was given to my stepsister Lynn, and I was moved to the maid's room in the basement. I told my friends I didn't mind. I trailed after Lynn, longing to play kid sister, but she too had read the story and she had the stepsister dialogue down pat. "Don't bother me," she snapped. "Stay away."

More and more, I did just that. As often as I could, two or three nights a week, I set up sleepovers at friends' houses. At age fifteen, I volunteered as a candy striper at the Peninsula General Hospital and sometimes slept there. I became a volunteer aide at the Neponsit Home for the Aged, and sometimes spent nights there too.

A wall went up, and I hid my feelings behind it. With friends, I was a happy, laughing girl; nothing seemed to bother me. But the real me, whoever that was, was off-limits. An important part of me was always withheld, sequestered in a secret territory, defended with a "No Trespassing" sign. Alone again, abandoned again, I tried to fit myself into other people's families. But I did not want to risk getting hurt again. My survival technique was to get close, but not too close.

At home, I drew criticism like a magnet draws iron filings. In the gospel according to Blanche, I made too much noise, I drank too much milk, and I caused too much trouble. I was blamed for everything that was broken, everything that was spilled, everything that was wrong. If I denied it, Blanche would turn to my father and say, "Larry, that girl is lying."

He did not defend me. He did not intervene. "He's being a good Jewish husband," I explained to myself. In our neighborhood, that meant earning a good living and letting the wife run the home and family.

"That girl is running wild," Blanche told him. I wasn't smoking, drinking, or doing drugs; I did have a boyfriend, but all we'd done was kiss, and I could count the number of those kisses on one hand. "She's messing around," Blanche said. "God only knows what she's up to." If I protested, she would turn to my father with the clincher. "Larry," she'd say, "that girl is lying."

I wasn't a liar, but who in the world was I? My identity was becoming an urgent question. I had few clues. While Bea was still alive, a Christian Science friend of hers, a woman I called Aunt Anna, told me that she had found me for my parents and arranged our meeting at the Fountainbleu Hotel in Miami Beach. She seemed to know about my birth parents. She told me that they were married, that they were good people and that I had brothers and sisters, some older than me, some younger. Bea was furious with Aunt Anna for having told me even this little bit. It ended their long friendship, and she made her swear not to say anything else. Even after Bea's death, when I called Aunt Anna with questions, she kept that promise.

In the library, I found a book on how adoptees can search for their birth parents, and tried to follow the instructions. I was confused, hurting, thinking childish thoughts. If Larry no longer wanted me, maybe there was some other father, or some other mother, who might want to take me back. I wrote to the Bureau of Vital Statistics in New York, asking for information, but they had no record of my birth or adoption. I wrote to Florida, the state where my parents and I had been brought together, but they too had no record of my existence. For the time being, I was at a dead end.

At home, tension was building. "I can't handle that girl," Blanche complained to my father. "She's too much for me." Once or twice, he did try to defend me. Now and then, they fought about me. One winter night, I was in my room, undressing for bed, when I overheard a particularly heated argument.

Suddenly, Blanche exploded. "That's it! I've had it!" she announced. "I'm leaving!" And she strode out the red front door, slamming it behind her.

Slumped in his chair, my father looked pale and defeated. "Don't worry, Daddy," I told him. "I'll go after her." He was one of those men who has to be married, and I understood that he needed a wife more than he needed a daugher. "I promise, Daddy," I said. "I'll get her back for you."

Outside, the trees hung heavy with snow that was still falling. I was barefoot, in a tee-shirt and underpants, running up and down the street, calling Blanche's name. There was no one in sight. Then I remembered Fran Miller, Blanche's only real friend in the neighborhood, and I raced to her house.

Wet and shivering, I waited for the door to open. Fran led me to the living room where Blanche was standing, her feet planted, her face still red with anger, her eyes challenging me from behind those strong glasses. "Blanche, please," I began. I was crying. "Please go back to my father." I was begging. "He loves you. He needs you." Hands on hips, she stared at me and, suddenly, I knew what she wanted to hear. "I promise that I'll stay away. If you go back, I won't bother you anymore."

Blanche went back to my father. Neither of us ever told him about what had happened on that snowy night, but I kept my promise.

I'd been staying away, but now I was truly gone. At sixteen, I was homeless. I bounced from one friend's house to another's, staying for a week or so at a time. Though I didn't realize it until years later, the other mothers were making the arrangements, passing me around among them. I had taken a course to become a Certified Nursing Assistant, and I earned whatever money I needed by working after school at the hospital or the old-age home.

I no longer had a key to what used to be "Yvette's house." Once a month or so, I'd check with the maid. If Blanche was at the beauty parlor, if it was safe, I'd come by to pick up fresh clothes. Now and then, I'd run into Larry. "Yvette, why don't you come home?" he asked, but I couldn't tell him about my promise to Blanche. "Things will be different," he said, but we both knew better than that.

At the end of my senior year in high school, though, Blanche herself tracked me down, calling different friends' houses until she found me, and asked me to come home. "I have something to tell you," she said. I had to ring the bell to get in, and then she led me to the living room, where my father was waiting.

"Your father and I are going to do something wonderful for you," she announced. I waited, wondering what she was up to now.

"We're going to give you a great opportunity," she continued. "We're sending you to Israel."

"What?" It took a moment for it to sink in. Then I smiled. And I agreed. I'd always been ready and eager for adventure. I figured that I'd explore my Jewish roots. I'd see the land of my ancestors, or the people I believed were my ancestors.

But I also understood. People were talking. My home-lessness was a neighborhood scandal. I was an embarass-ment, and Blanche was dealing with that by shipping me off to Israel. She meant it as a good riddance, but I was grateful. She could have chosen Outer Mongolia, and I'd have gone there too.

Before I could leave, though, I needed a passport. To get that, I needed a birth certificate. As I told my father, I'd already tried New York and Florida, both with no success.

He hesitated. "Utah," he said finally. "Try Salt Lake City, Utah."

I wrote to the Bureau of Vital Statistics in that city. In answer, I received a greenish piece of paper, a "Certificate of Live Birth" for Yvette Deborah Silverman, born August 20, 1955 in Salt Lake City.

There were no parents' names on that document, and no further information. And as I now know, the date was wrong.

CHAPTER 5

In the file folders packed away in the horse trailer that we were hauling across the country, there was the computer printout of an e-mail from a stranger. "Are you my sister?" he wanted to know. He had read about me, and he thought he might be my missing twin brother.

The message arrived when we were getting ready to leave Maine, and it thrilled me. "Dickie," I yelled, "listen to this." But it also scared me. Was this it? The final piece of my puzzle? All the mixed emotions came flooding back, the wanting-to-know and the being-afraid-to-know, the high hopes and then the dead ends.

I had set up a battered desk in the corner of the living room in Palmyra and, like Pac-Man, I was gradually eating up my surroundings, spreading out, surrounded now by stacks of papers that represented so many years of searching. A CB crackled in the background, the lifeline we used instead of the more expensive rural telephone. It was my connection to Dickie, our special way of keeping in constant touch. Two or three times an hour, he'd call to let me know where he was, and to ask if there was anything I needed. He was on and off in a flash, never saying anything sweet or silly, but it was a taciturn man's way of telling me that he cared. My moniker, chosen because it was catchy, not because it meant anything at the time, was Cherokee.

I sat at my installment-plan computer, and I tried not to expect too much. That has always been my psychic sun-screen, my protection against being burned again, being dis-appointed again. I keyed in an answer to the stranger, responding with my own careful questions. "Where were you born? When were you adopted? What do you know about it?"

His first answers came the next day, and a shiver of excitement ran through me. His data seemed to connect with my own story. His parents, or the people he called his par-ents, lived in New Jersey now. But when he was an infant, they'd been in Arizona and also Utah, the right part of the country for them to have found and adopted my brother. He didn't know the exact date of his birth, but that too seemed to match; maybe it had been changed, just like mine.

I wondered how long he'd been looking for his family. My own search had taken most of my lifetime. The Navajos have a saying: *Naninagoo hazho'ogo adaa ahoninidzingo ninima.* Walk in harmony within the universe by being aware of who you are. I was trying to do that, trying hard. But it can be complicated for people like me and that e-mail stranger, people who are still trying to figure out where they came from and where they belong.

Who am I? In search of answers, I spent long years fol-lowing a trail of false clues, bits and pieces of misinforma-tion that had been left behind to cover up the stealing of a child. To this day, I have still not found any adoption pa-pers, but I do have a collection of three birth certificates, each different from the other, none of them true.

The first one, sent for before I left for Israel, provided a starting place, a city of birth, and a wrong date. A few years later, I had a child of my own, born of a bad first marriage, a mistake that lasted just long enough to produce a son. I gave Bradley the same initial as Bea, naming him after her, in the Jewish tradition of keeping her memory and her spirit alive.

Suddenly, as I held little Brad in my arms, the search seemed more urgent than ever. I wanted to know what blood ran through his veins, and what genes shaped him. I needed answers for the questions that doctors were already asking, questions about his family medical history.

I wrote again to Salt Lake City and a second birth certificate arrived. This one added the name of the hospital, Salt Lake General. With that new clue, I hired a private detective, hoping he could find out more about my heritage and Brad's. "Lady, there must be some mistake," he reported back. "You can't have been born in that hospital. I've checked the records. There were no female children born there on your birth date."

A few years later, without realizing that I was sending him up that same blind alley, I hired a second private detective. He went a step further, checking the hospital records for eight days before my supposed birth date and five days after. There were no female children born there during that time period. I'd told the detective that I thought I had a twin brother, the boy Larry had told me he really wanted, but there were no twins born there on those dates either, only three boys who went home with their parents. The hospital itself had burned to the ground, but the microfilm records still existed, and the detective searched them to find the name of the doctor who was in charge of the maternity ward.

With that extra bit of information, I wrote for a third birth certificate. This was the most complete yet, "the one they could have sent in the first place," I thought, "if they weren't trying to hide something." Along with my name, the hospital, the date and time of birth, this certificate named Bea and Larry as the mother and father. And it was signed by two doctors, the head of the maternity ward and the resident who delivered me, Dr. Dean Day. I found his phone number and called him, and for a quick, thrilling moment, I thought I had also found myself.

"I remember you," he told me. "You were the first baby I ever delivered. I have the file. Call me back and I'll get it for you." When I called back, though, he was full of apologies. "I have all of your information in front of me," he said, "but I can't give it to you. I'm sorry. It's supposed to be sealed. I wish I could help you, but I can't." And there I was, in familiar territory again, at still another dead end.

Dr. Day was a lingering mystery. What reason did he have to lie? As I know now, he couldn't have delivered me. Why did he say he remembered me? As I've since learned, I wasn't born in a hospital; I was born in a lean-to in the middle of a cornfield. Three years ago, when I was still searching, I called his number again and spoke to his wife. "Did you call some years back?" she asked. She told me the doctor had died of cancer. "But he used to think about you," she said. "You were always on his mind, though I don't know why." Maybe he was part of the coverup. Maybe he had confused me with a different baby girl. I'll never know.

That was it. False leads and blind alleys. "You're nobody's baby," I told myself. "But so what?" I was married to Dickie by now, and we had two wonderful daughters. I had my son Brad, and Dickie had six children by a former marriage, all of them in and out of our house, the great big family I'd always dreamed of. And when I wanted mothering, there was Dickie's big-hearted mom, living just down the road.

"Get on with it, Yvette," I kept telling myself. "Forget the search."

Like me, my Navajo family was also being led down false trails. Early on, a Social Services official waved a paper at them, signed with my mother's name, stating that she had given up her missing twins for adoption. But my mother could not have signed her name. She could not speak, read, or write English. It was a forgery. Later, they were shown another paper, this one signed with my mother's "mark." In my mother's generation, many Indians signed with a simple symbol or ideogram, "making their mark," as they called it. But this was not the mark that my mother used. It was another forgery. My family was shown still a third paper, this one signed with a thumbprint. They compared it with my mother's actual thumbprint and, once again, they had a mismatch.

Along the way, my family heard of money changing hands. They were told of a nurse who'd been paid to help spirit away the twins. But these leads, like the forgeries, always trailed away into dead ends.

Then, in 1995, a computer arrived in the old white farmhouse that Dickie and I called home, and it changed everything. At the time, I was driving back and forth to the University of Maine in Augusta, taking a heavy load of courses for a degree in psychology. I was staying there until all hours of the night, using the library computer to research and write my course papers. I couldn't keep doing that, not with a family waiting for me at home, but there was no way I could afford to buy a computer of my own. Then I heard about a correspondence course in computing, a series of lessons that cost fifty dollars a month, a sum I could manage, and included a computer that would be mine to keep.

I signed up, and the computer was delivered, a door to the future, a key to my past. After a few months, I saved up enough to add a modem, my connection to the Internet.

And, with that, I was deep in cyberspace, via America Online. I discovered that you could download free computer games, and I did that. After hours of study, when I'd feel my mind cramping, I'd relax with a game or two. Dickie hated that computer, resenting the time I spent on it. He was jealous of the games I played, jealous of the little man with red hair who climbed up and down a digital ladder. It became a family joke. "Hey, Dad," Heather used to tease, "Mommy's playing with that man again."

By year's end, I turned serious, no longer typing in "games," but keying in a different word: "adoption." The screen filled with a long list of adoption subjects. It told me I could search state by state, and I clicked on the best clue I had: Utah.

I read the messages that other people had posted, so many of them. Grown children were searching for their mothers and fathers; parents were looking for the sons and daughters they'd once given up. "Does it work?" I wondered. "Do they ever find one another?"

I added a message of my own: *"Born Aug. 20, 1955, Salt Lake City. Female. Looking for birth family or siblings."*

There were no answers. I kept reading other people's messages, but none seemed to match my vital statistics. And then, one day, there it was. *"Looking for a set of twins,"* the message said, *"born in 1950's. Contact Sue Stevens."*

I e-mailed her, explaining that I was a twin and giving my birth date. We began to exchange messages back and forth. Sue was a good Samaritan, a kind stranger who was not searching for herself, just helping a woman she'd heard about, a woman who'd been searching for years for her lost siblings but had no computer of her own. "Any background?" Sue asked me. "Any birthmarks? Any medical history?" I answered with bits and pieces of my story and, with each message, my excitement grew. E-mail was dazzling; it arrived in a nanosecond; it brought instant answers to the questions of a lifetime.

My heart pounded as I read Sue's messages. She told me that this woman's family had traced their lost twins from Utah to Florida. They had lost all traces of the boy in Florida, but they had followed the girl north to Brooklyn, New York, then lost track of her there. I could barely believe the sentences I was scrolling through. It was an amazing match, a mirror image of my own history.

I had followed that same route. I knew that, somehow, I'd been taken from Utah to Florida. That's where I'd first met Bea and Larry. That's where we returned for a couple of weeks each winter, back where we started at the Fountainbleu Hotel. I had a special playmate in Florida, a little boy who was always there at the same time as we were. People used to stop us as we played hide-and-seek in the hotel corridors. "Is that your brother?" they'd ask me. Sometimes, wishing it were so, I'd giggle and say yes.

My first home with Bea and Larry was in Brooklyn. Had this woman's family located me there? Had they then lost track of me when we moved to "Yvette's house" in Neponsit? I was giddy with hope, but then it faded fast. A new e-mail arrived from Sue. "This woman is a Navajo," she told me.

"No way," I wrote back. "I'm white. I'm Jewish. I'm not an Indian. I don't even know what an Indian is." Sue answered with a birthdate, September 10, 1953, but that didn't fit with my three birth certificates. "It's not me," I told her. Sue wrote that the twins were born in Arizona, but that too didn't match my Utah birth certificates. She e-mailed me information about the stolen Indian children, about Utah as a clearinghouse for those children, about birth certificates that were changed. "No way," I repeated. "It's not me. I'm white and I'm Jewish."

I resisted. I fought the idea. But Sue kept passing along

messages from the woman she was trying to help. "No way," I kept telling her. "It's not me."

Still, I couldn't get it out of my mind. I typed "Indian" into the computer, and got back a lecture on political correctness. I tried "Native American" and read the entries on history and background. And there was something else. Under *"Native American,"* it said. *"See Lost Bird Network."*

Clicking on that, I found the story of the first Lost Bird, *Zintkala Nuni,* and a special site for missing Indian children. There, I read the excerpts from Renee Sansom-Flood's heartbreaking book, *Lost Bird of Wounded Knee: Spirit of the Lakota.* There, I began to exchange messages with Marie Fouche, the woman who now runs the Lost Bird Web page. She told me still more about stolen Indian children. "It's possible," she wrote in an e-mail. "That woman could be your sister." But that was not what I wanted to read on my computer screen.

It was too strange, too weird. "Help me out here, God," I prayed. "Tell me it isn't so." But the more I said no, the louder the little voice was in the back of my head, an echo that said maybe. By now, Sue had let slip who the woman was, Lora Chee of Page, Arizona. I couldn't stop thinking about it. I couldn't sleep. I wanted to settle things with that woman. "I know you're looking for your siblings," I wanted to tell her, "but I'm not it. I'm white and I'm Jewish."

I called information, but her number was unlisted. "This woman is looking for her lost sister," I told the operator. "And I could be her," I said. In my mind, that was a lie, but I was trying to make it as urgent and dramatic as I could. "Please help. Please ask her to call me back collect at this number."

Five minutes later, the phone rang. With the time difference, it was four A.M. in Arizona but Lora, wakened from a deep sleep, had called back. We talked for a long time that night, me in my fast New York style, she in her slow Navajo way, and I liked her from the very first minute. We talked again and again, running up phone bills that neither of us could afford.

"My mother never stopped looking for her children," Lora told me. She talked of how her mother had become obsessed with the missing twins, losing touch with her harmony. Even when she was dying of cancer, she kept up the search. On her death bed, she made her daughters promise to keep looking for them. It was all she had to bequeath, a search that was passed from her oldest daughters down to Lora, her youngest one.

Lora told me about her own search, endless calls to the Navajo Tribal office, Social Services, and Bureaus of Vital Statistics. "I made so many long-distance calls that my phone was disconnected for a while, until I could pay the bill." She began to place ads in Arizona and Utah newspapers and in the *Navajo Times*. "I got a lot of answers, letters of sympathy, because almost every Indian family has someone missing. Some of those people even sent me money, a dollar or two to help with the search."

Among the letters she received was one from Sue Stevens, offering a different kind of help. Using her computer, Sue downloaded the names and addresses of all the people in the United States with the same family name as the twins had been born with. Lora used the money she'd received, all $65 of it, to buy stamps and begin sending letters to those people.

The letters brought some answers, but not the one Lora had been hoping for, and she realized that the lost twins had probably had their names changed. Then Sue explained to her that the missing children weren't likely to be on or near the reservation, reading the papers where her ads were running. Instead, Sue had another idea, and she offered to post a message on the Internet.

"I wasn't sure what the Internet was, but all that month, every time the phone rang, my heart jumped," Lora remembered. "All that month, I had a strange feeling that someone special was going to call me. I told my husband about it, and he just laughed. 'Sure,' he said. 'A bill collector.' And when the telephone operator told me that a lady from Maine was calling, I thought, 'Wow, those bill collectors in Maine sure get up early.'"

For two weeks, Lora and I talked almost every other day. On one call, she began to tell me about her family's medical history. Her mother had died of esophogeal cancer. "It happened eight years ago," she told me, and for a moment I found it hard to breathe. Eight years ago, I'd been sick with that same cancer, a terrible disease that was rare in women. I had massive doses of radiation implants, and I had to push away my own daughters, afraid to contaminate them, afraid to hug or kiss them.

I was given three to six months to live, and it threw Dickie into a tailspin. When we married, I'd made him swear to stay sober. It wasn't easy for him, but he'd kept that vow, another of his gruff ways of showing his love for me. Now, faced with the possibility of losing me, looking for escape in the bottom of a bottle, he started drinking again.

It's strange but, in a way, that saved my life. I couldn't die; I couldn't leave Heather and Lori with a father who was getting drunk every night; I couldn't leave Brad, my restless, needy boy, with a man who might turn away from him. At that moment, I had no one else, no sister or good friend, to entrust my children to. I found myself getting angry. I knew what it was like to watch a mother wasting away. I knew what it was like to be left behind, with no one to love you or look after you, and I was not going to let that happen to a child of mine.

And so I said no to death. As if I had a choice, I made up my mind to live. And somehow, to the doctors' amazement, the cancer went into remission. Five years later, I was still symptom-free and pronounced cured.

In those same years, I'd also found a cure for Dickie's return to alcoholism. "Here are the divorce papers," I told him, waving them at him. "I'm keeping them in my drawer. I love you, but I'll use them if you ever get drunk again."

Lora kept talking about medical histories. She told me that hyperactivity ran in her family, and that had always been one of my son Brad's problems. She said her family had also experienced an enzyme problem, similar to Heather's. "Interesting," I thought. "Coincidences," I told myself. "But no way!"

We compared dates, and it became stranger and stranger, more and more like a Tony Hillerman mystery. The years when her family had traced their missing sister to Utah, to Florida, and then to Brooklyn were the same years that I'd been in those places. The coincidences were mounting up, but neither of us yet believed that we were sisters. Both of us were wary. We shared dates, places, and other bits and pieces of information, but neither of us wanted to say too much. Each of us was waiting for the other one to come up with something that would prove or, as I expected, disprove it. Lora kept talking about her family, but she never named their names.

"Look for papers," she kept telling me. "If you find any papers, read them to me." She called one afternoon as I was trying to organize my overflowing files, the stacks of correspondence and e-mail printouts, the children's school reports, the household bills and receipts. I had a big box of papers on my lap and, as we were talking, it slid to the floor. "Dammit!" I said. When Lora wanted to know what was going on, I explained that I'd just dropped a box of papers that an aunt had sent me after my adoptive father died, and now they were all over the floor.

"Pick it all up," she told me. "Read what you've got. Read it to me." I gathered up the papers and began reading. Bea had kept every letter I wrote to her from sleepaway camp, and I read one of them to Lora. "Dear Mom," I read, "I like it here at camp . . ."

Then there was a plastic bag with other papers in it, some bills and two pages torn from a spiral notebook. Those pages were covered with strange words in Bea's handwriting, some of it in ink, some in pencil, some in green crayon, as if she'd been making notes at different times, on different phone calls.

"What is it?" Lora asked.

"It's nothing," I told her. "I've read all this stuff before. I've read it over and over, and it makes no sense."

But she insisted. The handwritten words were meaningless to me, but I read them to her.

"Betty Jackson . . ." I read. "Tolani Lake . . . September 10, 1953."

"Oh my God," she said.

"Yazzie Monroe . . ." I continued reading.

"Oh my God," she said again.

There was something about six feet two and a date, June 26, 1930. And some mysterious numbers.

"Oh my God," she kept saying. I knew she had young children, and I thought one of them might have fallen and hurt himself. "Is everything all right?" I asked. "Are you okay?"

"Oh my God, it's you," she said. "You're my sister." Her voice, usually so calm, was cracking with emotion. "Read it again," she said. "Read the names again." And so for a second time, I read the handwritten names.

"Betty Jackson is our mother," she told me. She was laughing. She was crying. She asked me to wait while she wiped away the tears. "Yazzie Monroe, he is our father. Six feet two is how tall he is. June 26, 1930 is his birth date. Tolani Lake is where our family has always lived."

My own heart was pounding. "You're my sister," she was saying. My heart was beating so loud that I thought she must be hearing it at the other end of the phone. Is that why I was shouting? "No, Lora," I said. "Wait, Lora." I kept trying to interrupt, trying to say it must be a mistake, but she wasn't listening to me.

"You're my sister," she kept saying. She asked if there was anything else on the paper, and I read her the string of mysterious numbers.

"One oh nine, dash, three eight eight. And one oh nine, dash, three eight nine."

"Yes!" said Lora. She was jubilant. "Yes! Those are the census numbers for the twins," she said, explaining that they were the Navajo version of Social Security numbers, a way of identifying everyone who belonged to the tribe. "It's you!" she said. "After all these years, I've found my sister."

When Lora hung up the phone, as she told me later on, she was crying. She got dressed and went to work. "But I couldn't stop crying," she told me. "And then I couldn't stop laughing. 'Oh, my God,' I kept thinking. 'It's her!' Everyone at work thought I was going crazy. I couldn't stop crying and laughing, and my boss had to send me home early."

At my end, when I hung up the phone, I was shaking. This wasn't what I'd expected. This wasn't what I'd been searching for. I still felt that it had to be some mistake. Or some coincidence. Maybe the paper was about some other little girl whom Bea and Larry had thought about adopting, someone not "special" enough, someone they looked at before they found me.

I didn't know what to think. I looked in the mirror and my face hadn't changed. It was still a white face, still a Jewish face.

"It's crazy," I told Dickie. "I am not that woman's sister." He gave me one of his long looks. "Don't be so sure, Yvette," he said. "I've always thought you had some Indian blood in you." If that was true, I wanted to know why he hadn't said anything about it before. Dickie laughed out loud. "C'mon, Yvette," he said. "You always had that Jewish beanie planted on your head. No one could tell you anything different."

I kept fighting the idea, but Lora and I also kept talking. A couple of my other sisters also called to talk to me. No one, though, said anything to our father. He had closed the subject; he had told Lora: "I don't want to talk on this search anymore." Then, by mail, I sent them a photograph and, as Lora told me later on, our father saw it. He looked at it and then, without a word, he walked out of the house. Many weeks later, when the question was more settled, Lora talked to him.

"We have found your daughter," she told him.

"I know," he said. He was not a man who wasted words. "Now bring her home."

In our little town of Palmyra, Maine, news traveled quickly. A local newspaper heard about it and wrote a story about a Jewish woman who'd found her Indian family. NBC-TV read about it and invited Lora and me to come to New York for a news segment. I was still resisting the idea, but I wanted to meet this woman who said she was my sister. When I saw her in New York, I didn't think she looked anything like me. She brought pictures of my father and of Aunt Despah, and our NBC guide thought I looked a bit like them. I disagreed. I thought I was unlike anyone in that Navajo family, but in small, odd ways Lora and I were echos of one another. We liked the same things; we laughed at the same jokes; without consultation, we ordered the same midnight treats from the hotel room service.

Meanwhile, officials at the Navajo Nation were checking things out. I still had my doubts, but they looked at the evidence and thought I was a daughter of the tribe. They wanted to welcome me home, and they sent plane tickets for me and Dickie, Heather, and Lori. We traveled to Arizona, and the pile of coincidences grew to a mountain of proof. Everyone was convinced. Everyone but me.

I still resisted the idea. Who am I? I'd been asking that question for so many years, but this wasn't the answer I expected. "Send me some of your clothes," Lora suggested. "I'll give them to a medicine man. He'll pray over them, and he'll know if you are my sister."

I shook my head in amazement. I was a rational woman. I didn't believe, not yet anyway, in that kind of magic. But I packed up a worn headband and a pair of old socks, and mailed them to Arizona. A couple of weeks later, Lora called. The medicine man had said yes. "Come home," Lora urged. She sounded so certain. "Come home soon."

Dickie and I talked late into the night. Should we go? Should we stay? If we went ahead, what would we have to leave behind? If we stayed, what would we miss out on? We weighed the familiar against the unknown, an old way of life against a new one.

Blood ties pulled me west, where I had a family to gain. Dickie, though, had a family to lose. His roots were in Maine, and they ran deep. His parents were there, his siblings, his children, and now even a couple of grandchildren. As he drove the country roads, every face he saw was familiar, every house he passed held a memory. As much as I wanted to go, it had to be Dickie's decision. He sat on the faded couch in our Palymra farmhouse and, after a long silence, told me what was on his mind.

"You've been spending your life with my family," he said. "Now it's time to spend it with yours."

I felt weak in the knees. Dickie was not a romantic man, not the kind who brings flowers or chocolates, but this was the most loving thing that anyone had ever offered to do for me. I leaned over to hug him, but Dickie wasn't finished. "I'm not going to live to be very old," he was saying. I turned away now, not wanting to hear those blunt words.

But we'd both heard them before, from his doctors. Dickie was a taciturn man, embarrassed by emotions, but when it counted, he was a loving and generous man. "I want you to be with your own people," he went on. "They'll take care of you. They'll take care of the girls."

We'd scouted the territory on that first visit, me and Dickie, Heather and Lori. But moving in is different from just passing through. Even after the decision was made, we had second thoughts. Even after we were on the road, Dickie and I were still going round and round on those questions. Do we really want this? When we arrive on their doorstep, will they, my lost-and-found family, really want us?

Just before we left Palmyra, there were more messages from that e-mail stranger. The story began to fall apart. He wanted to be my missing brother, but there were more differences than coincidences. The more he told me, the less anything meshed. His parents swore that he was their natural child, not an adopted one. He tore their house apart, hunting for evidence and finding none. "But I don't look anything like my sister," he told me. He sent a picture, and he didn't look anything like me or anyone in my family either.

It was a mistake. One false lead down. How many more to go? Ahead of us, waiting at Lora's house, was a collection of messages from another stranger, another possibility, another man looking for his lost family. He had heard about us and written to Lora. "Are you my sister?" he asked. "Am I your brother?"

I could not stop hoping that, one day, the answer would be yes. The Navajos believed that everything happened in its own right time. Was it, then, time for my lost brother to be found, to be touched, to be welcomed home?

CHAPTER 6

W e arrived in a cloud of dust, which is how you arrive anywhere on the high-and-dry desert of Tolani Lake. Not much grows here, not much keeps the arid earth in place. It blows and churns, moves and shifts, erodes in the wind and changes shape. Forever morphing, just like me.

We pulled up to my sister Katie's house, and relatives tumbled out to meet us. We were surrounded by sisters and brothers, nephews, nieces and cousins. Ya'at eh's, the Navajo greeting, all around. Hugs and handshakes all around. Some tears and much laughter.

Katie led us into her house, a structure of wood frame and poured concrete, its outer skin turning pale pink in the glow of a setting sun. It was low-slung and utilitarian, with the pitched roof typical of the homes the tribe has been building to replace the old hogans. "You'll stay here with me," said Katie, and that was that. She was the family's second-born, but as the eldest of the siblings still living in Tolani, she was the mother-hen to all the others. Dark eyes shining in a round face, strong hands smoothing my hair, she was an open-hearted woman, and strong on the Navajo tradition that you always had a plate of food and a place to sleep for anyone who needed it.

We'd camp in with Katie until we could find a place of our own to rent. She was a prim woman, a schoolteacher by profession, her clothes crisp and well-pressed, her house always in order. My own clothes were rumpled, my own life disorderly. But as different as we were, Katie was destined to become my closest sister.

"Our father will be here tomorrow," she told me. Following the tradition for Navajo men, he had come to Tolani Lake to live with his wife's clan after their marriage. Now, a widower at age sixty-seven, he was moving back and forth between an old hogan on my mother's land and his own ranch, some distance away in his home village of Kabito, where he still ran cattle, sheep, and goats. "He's bringing a sheep for a cookout," Katie said. "We'll have a big feast in your honor."

We stayed up talking until after midnight, eager to catch up on one another's lives. Among Navajos, I knew it was wrong to look too long in anyone's eyes, but I couldn't help myself. It was impolite to stare, but I was so excited, so curious. I studied one face and then another, drinking in the look of my family, hunting for little resemblances between them and me. Katie's daughter DiDi, the same age as my Heather, looked nothing like my daughter. The best I could do was Darlena's nose which, I decided, was a lot like mine.

I was amazed at being there. "Think of it," I said. "If I hadn't been on the Internet, I'd still be out there. Like a lost bird," I smiled. I rattled on. "If Sue Stevens hadn't had a good heart and offered to help Lora, I'd never have found you."

Darlena, born a couple of years after I went missing, listened patiently. She was a modern Navajo woman, working in Flagstaff as a police officer, living in Tolani during the week and then commuting on weekends to her own home and family in another corner of the rez. But she held to traditional etiquette. It was rude to interrupt, no matter what someone was saying, no matter how long they took to say it. When she was sure I had finished, Darlena shook her head. "No, Yvette, you're wrong."

She said it softly, with a smile, because Navajos don't like to disagree. "You didn't do it by being on the Internet. That was just a tool that the Holy People used," she explained. "We prayed to them, and they heard us. And Sue Stevens didn't do it either. She was another instrument for the Holy People, the good heart that they worked through."

It was a long speech for Darlena. It was a different way of thinking about things. "Oh, well, okay," I said. "I see." But I didn't really see. As I fell into bed that night, I wasn't sure if I wanted to think that way. And even if I wanted to, I didn't know if I could bend my brain and my stubborn will to the Navajo way.

I said the *Shema*. I'd been told that Navajos were ecumenical, and that many of them followed two or even three religions. Some believed in the old ways but also took part in the peyote rites of the Native American Church, a newer religion that came from the Plains Indians and was adopted by people in many different tribes. Some were traditional Navajos but also attended a Protestant or Catholic or Mormon church. "I follow the Jesus road," one man had told me. For the moment, still searching for intersections, I was the only one following yet another road, the Moses road.

I woke the next morning in a strange bed in a strange place. The sky was blue and cloudless, with the last streaks of the sunrise, ribbons of pink and yellow, still lingering on the eastern horizon. "It's past seven o'clock," Katie told me, big sister making me feel like a slug-a-bed. Like any good Navajo, she had risen with the dawn, stepping outside to face the rising sun, say her prayers, and sprinkle a bit of corn pollen.

Before long, our father's old pickup came chugging up to the house and my daughters were instantly at his side, his adoring bookends. He was usually quiet, impassive, his feelings hidden, his face shadowed by the tall crown and rolled brim of a pressed-straw hat, a version of the old cowboy hat that people called "a reservation hat." That day, with his hat pushed back on his head, I could see the satisfied smile on his broad face and the warm shine of pleasure in his dark eyes. "Welcome home to my daughter," he said in Navajo, his voice slow and deep. "Welcome to Dickie, who is my new son. Welcome to my granddaughters."

It was instant family, like instant coffee. We talked, some in English, some in Navajo. We laughed, no translations needed. I was among people who were still strangers, but I felt at home. I worried that it felt too good, too right, too comfortable. I thought there had to be another shoe, waiting to drop. But meanwhile, I couldn't stop smiling. "Yvette, you look silly," Dickie teased. "Quit grinning so much." But, for those first few days at least, he was doing it too.

I stood in the backyard of Katie's house, watching the preparations for the feast, adjusting to the taste of a Navajo. My father killed the sheep like a kosher butcher, slitting its throat. The animal was skinned and then cut into rib sections and loins for grilling over an outdoor fire. When we gathered to eat, people vied for the fattest pieces, as if cholesterol were just a white man's worry.

Fry bread was a part of the feast, a part of every traditional Navajo meal. It is a mix of flour and water, with a dash of baking powder, giving you a flat bread, something like a pita, but crunchy and dotted with air bubbles. If you wanted to, you could make it lower-cal by cooking it on a red-hot griddle or skillet. My clan, though, preferred it deep-fried. Oil and fat, the more saturated the better, were really big on this reservation.

We ate, gossiping and laughing, until we could eat no more. But this was a well-planned Navajo feast, which meant that there was enough left over to send everyone home with a package of meat.

After the feast, when we could move again, we climbed into vans and pickups, following the paved road to a yellow gate that marked the cattle-crossing. Then we turned onto the washboard roads that led to my mother's old ranch. All that was left of her old house was the cracked foundation slab. What stood at the ranch now was a cluster of structures, "an outfit," as they called it. There was a flat-roofed house where a nephew now lived with his family, and a small shed that Robert, my bachelor brother, sometimes used as a crash pad. There was a brush arbor, the shaded Navajo lanai. There was an unused, half-collapsed corral and a falling-down sheep pen.

Most important, there was the family hogan, the traditional hut made of rough-hewn logs and covered these days with painted plywood panels instead of the old mud and twigs. This was the place where family ceremonies were held, but my father stayed here during visits to Tolani, and Darlena also used it sometimes as her home away from home. It was a one-room structure, with a gas stove pushed against one wall and beds against another. The cross-beams were the shelves that held groceries and dishes. The dirt floor was covered with strips of carpet, except for a center circle of bare earth where a fire had now been lit, the only light in a hogan still without electricity.

We gathered in the hogan, a Navajo mix of the secular and the religious, the common and the uncommon. It was an octagon topped with a domed roof that provided the roundness, the sacred shape among the Navajos. If you sit or stand or dance in a circle, you are united with everyone else who is within it. A circle is outside of time, with no beginning and no end. The entrance was a door that faced east, toward the rising sun.

East, toward Jerusalem, was a Jewish direction too, and the circle was a shape that brought back Jewish memories. Grandma Sophie used to tell me about long-ago weddings when the groom would walk in a circle around the bride for a mystical seven times. She explained that, by tradition, the wedding ring was supposed to be a plain, unbroken band of gold, with no beginning and no end, a symbol of the eternal cycle or circle of life. She used to begin every Passover seder meal with a hard-boiled egg, explaining that its roundness was a similar symbol. For Jewish mystics, the circle is a sign of protection and a reference to God, who is sometimes called "the one with no beginning and no end."

Once, long ago, I sat in a synagogue and heard the rabbi ask all of those in need of healing prayers to come forward and stand in "a circle of love." Now, with my Navajo family, I was part of such a circle, sitting around the fire of the hogan, a small hole in the roof drawing away the smoke.

My father was a *hataali,* a singer or medicine man who could perform the traditional ceremonies or chantways. Once there had been dozens of such ceremonies, but only eleven or so were still remembered and in common use these days. Some were brief, a matter of hours. Others were more complex chantways that could include hundreds of songs and last for days. One generation of medicine men passed the chantways to the next, an oral liturgy of sacred words and ritual melodies that could take years to study and memorize. Even after a long apprenticeship, an individual singer might acquire the knowledge of only one or two of the more complex chantways.

We sat cross-legged on cushions and sheepskins, forming a circle. My father sat facing the east, his *jish* at his side. It was a soft leather pouch that held his sacred items—some corn pollen and sage, talking sticks and eagle feathers, some wild mountain tobacco, and four small packages of earth that he had gathered from the four holy mountains.

My father began a small ceremony, a retelling of the story of the *Dineh*, the Navajo people, and where they came from. The chant was high-pitched and hypnotic, the rhythm insistent as a drumbeat, the melody rising and falling and rising again. My father sang in Navajo, and Darlena whispered a translation in my ear.

Archaeologists and anthropologists believe that the early Navajos drifted down from the north, from Alaska and Canada, and their language is somewhat similar to that of the original people who still live in the Northwest Territory. When they arrived in the southwest, they were nomads, hunters and gatherers, and also warriors. At times, they were landlocked pirates, raiding the herds of the neighboring Hopis and the Spaniards. Navajo is not a word in the *Dineh*'s language; it became the name that the world knows them by when, after they'd learned to plant corn, a neighboring tribe began to call them *Apache de Nabaho*, the people of the great planted fields, or the people of the earth.

But my father was singing a different song and telling a different story. "We came from under the earth," he was singing. In the beginning, the people lived in three underground worlds, each one different, each one remembered by its color—the Dark or Red World, the Blue World, and the Yellow World. My father chanted of Be'yocity, the child of the Sun, one of the First Beings, both male and female in one body. "Like a twin," I thought. "An unseparated twin." When the Third World was about to be destroyed by a great flood, Be'yocity saved the people by creating the Big Reed through which they emerged into the next world, the Fourth World. My father looked at me and smiled. "Be'yocity had light eyes," he said, "and golden hair."

When the people emerged through the Big Reed, they

found the Earth World, the one that was fo
marriage of Mother Earth and Father Sky. T
still in semidarkness, not yet the earth we know.
too, had a different form, and they could talk to the
who were their older, wiser brothers.

Then the Holy People helped the *Dineh* to plant four
sacred mountains, *Sisnaajinii* or Mount Blanca in the east,
Tsoodzil or Mount Taylor in the south, *Dook'o'sliid* or San
Francisco Peak in the west, and *Dibe Nitsaa* or Mount Herp-
erus in the north. And those became the borders of the *Di-
nehteh*, old Navajoland. The people needed light, and so the
Sun and Moon and Stars were arranged carefully in the sky
by the *yei*, or Holy People. But Coyote, the mischievous *yei*,
grew impatient. He took the blanket that held the last re-
maining stars and flung them into the heavens, to shine at
random in what white people call the Milky Way.

Next, the people needed fire, but Fire God did not want
to share it with them. Coyote, the trickster and trouble-
maker, waited until Fire God fell asleep; then he crept in
and stole some of the fire to give to the people. Then the
Holy People taught them how to live in the Earth World,
how to give thanks and how to take care of the animals
and the birds, the corn and the other plants that the *yei*
had created.

After that, Changing Woman was born of the darkness
and the dawn, of Mother Earth and Father Sky. She was
found sleeping on the side of a mountain, a rainbow over
her head, flowers all around her. Like me, she was
adopted—by First Man and First Woman. They watched
over her as she came of age, feeding her on sun-ray pollen,
pollen from the clouds and dew from the flowers, the holy
elements of fire, air, and water. She lived out the cycle of
the seasons—born in spring, coming of age in summer,
growing old in fall and dying in winter, only to be born
again when spring returned.

In that primal calendar, in nine days rather than nine months, Changing Woman gave birth to the Twin Hero Gods. Called Monster Slayer and Born for Water, they killed the monsters that roamed the earth. They made it safe for the first people who looked like us, a male and female created from ears of corn. But the Twin Gods had not managed to slay all the monsters. Poverty had escaped. So had Sickness and War. So had Death.

A Navajo sing is a story-telling, ritual words about the long-ago creation, a long chant to restore harmony in the present. This one touched something deep within me. I could feel the tension leaving my body. There were more clicks of recognition. I'd grown up with stories that were not so different—Noah surviving the flood, Prometheus stealing the fire. I remembered the biblical story of Adam created from a handful of dust, and Eve made from a rib. It was only a small leap of faith from them to the corn people, stirred into life in the same way, by the breath of the Great Spirit or the one God.

It was late when my father unfolded his long legs and stood up. We followed him out and stood under a starstruck sky, bright enough to show us the way to our vehicles with no need for torches or flashlights. I rode home without speaking, wanting to hold on to the warm feelings that were the beginning of being healed.

Suddenly the caravan of vans and pickups stopped. My father was in the lead, and the word was passed from vehicle to vehicle. In his headlights, he had seen two coyotes loping across our path. Climbing down from his pickup, he began to search for their tracks. The rest of us milled around, and Darlena explained what was happening. "Coyote is a messenger," she told me, "but his news is usually bad." Grownups tell funny stories to children about Coyote's mischief, so that the children won't be afraid, but grownups know that Coyote is always lurking and is always hungry.

I watched my father searching the side of the road until he found the tracks. I could hear him chanting a Navajo prayer as he erased the tracks. "So Coyote cannot find his way back to us," Darlena explained. Then my father waved and returned to his pickup. Protected from Coyote's bad news, it was now safe for us to go on.

The next day, without a word, my father was gone. Navajos make a ceremony of greeting everyone, saying *ya'at eh*. They go around the room, shaking everyone's hand. But the members of my family didn't seem to say good-bye. One minute they were there; the next minute, without a word, without a wave, they were gone. Maybe it was considered bad luck to say *ha'go'neh* or good-bye, but that would take some getting used to.

Every day, after the yellow bus had taken my daughters off to school, I explored the sandy paths of Tolani Lake. Everywhere I went, I was surrounded by relatives. Even people who were not connected to me by blood were related to me by clan, and they took those family ties seriously. They told me to look on them as stand-in mothers and fathers, loyal sisters and brothers, willing aunts and uncles. "What does my daughter need?" they asked. "How can I help my sister?" they wanted to know.

The worst thing you can say about a Navajo is this: "He acts as if he has no relatives." It means he's selfish, out only for himself, uncaring for his family. No one could ever say that about the extended family that I had lost and now found.

It was 1997, but Tolani Lake lived in a time zone of its own. Many of the conveniences I took for granted did not exist here. I kept looking around Katie's house. "Where's the phone?" I finally asked, and Katie laughed. She had no phone. A couple of my sisters and brothers had a phone from time to time, when they could manage the bills, but not just now. We were headed for the millennium, but three out of four Navajo homes still had no telephones.

"No problem," said Katie. I wanted to call Maine, to let everyone know that we'd arrived safely and to get news of the family Dickie and I had left behind. She led me down the road to the Tolani Chapter House, the community's heart and center, the town hall where tribal councils, once held around campfires, now took place. The only public phone booth in Tolani stood just outside that Chapter House.

Connections with the outside world were not easy. If I had a handbag-full of change, I could stand in that phone booth and make my call. If I didn't have enough coins to pour into the slots, I had to hope that someone would accept my call collect. If anyone out there wanted to place a call to me, it was an old-fashioned, two-step process. It was a throwback to a time Larry Silverman had told me about, when he was a boy in post-war Brooklyn, when phones were still a luxury, when people called you at the corner candy store. Half a century later, the phone that rang inside the Tolani Chapter House was like the one that used to ring in the candy store. The people there would take a message, and then pin it up on the bulletin board. As often as I could, as often as I remembered, I stopped by to check for any messages.

We were cut off from the world. No phone meant no Internet, no faxes, no more instant e-mails. If I wanted to send a letter by earth mail, it was fifty miles to buy postage stamps in Winslow. There was a small Trading Post in Tolani, where I could buy a loaf of bread or a tin of canned milk, but there were no other stores, no restaurants, no bowling alley or movie theater. There was a preschool and a senior-citizens center, the beginning and end of life taken care of, but those of us in the middle were on our own.

There was nothing happening here but, somehow, there was always something to do. This was a family where no one ever did anything alone. If a niece was driving to Flagstaff, she passed the word, checking to see who wanted to go along for the ride. There were family picnics, family outings, constant family gatherings and ceremonies.

A month after my arrival, I climbed into the van and pointed it toward Flagstaff. I was dressed in the only skirt I owned, a Navajo velveteen outfit, a gift from my father. "He never bought me anything like that," said Katie, and we both laughed at that flicker of sibling rivalry. Dickie and the girls stayed behind, victims of a flu epidemic that had hit the reservation. But I was headed for my first Navajo wedding, the marriage of Darlena's son Erikson.

I pulled up to a ceremonial hogan, round as always, but larger than the usual ones. My sister Lora was arriving at the same time. "What's a Navajo wedding like?" I asked her. "A lot of planning," she told me with a laugh. "A lot of work." Inside, we joined Darlena and our other sisters and brothers. At that point, only the groom's family were in the hogan, my father sitting up front, waiting to perform the ceremony.

A traditional Navajo wedding is "a promising to one another," as my sisters explained, an exchange of deeds as well as vows. "We have to wait," Darlena explained to me. "Our family has brought the gifts. Now we have to see if the bride's family accepts them."

As we waited, my sisters whispered stories of past marriages. "Poor Nettie," they said. In the tradition of the time, my eldest sister's marriage was an arranged one, an agreement between the bride's family and the groom's. Nettie had no voice in choosing her own husband, but she did have a say in whether to stay married. "Some years passed," Lora told me, "and then she put his saddle outside the door." That was it, divorce Navajo-style. She could have reopened the door, inviting him back into the marriage, but she never did.

The next sister, Katie, also had an arranged marriage but, though it had its problems, it was more successful. By Lora's wedding day, the tradition had changed, and she and Sam chose each other. Yet marriages were still not private affairs between a man and a woman; they were still arrangements that involved two families.

Outside the ceremonial hogan, the bride's family seemed to be taking a long time to contemplate the gifts. Those gifts were not for the bride. Instead, by Navajo tradition, some of the gifts were for her parents, and other gifts were for the aunts or clan mothers who'd helped to raise her. "I watched over this child. I taught her to weave," an aunt might say before a wedding, "and now I want a concha belt." Luckily for Darlena, this bride did not have too many aunts, and the bridal price had been set at four cattle, a silver-and-turquoise concha belt and some money.

More than an hour passed. Inside the hogan, the groom's family began to fidget. At the last minute, the bride's family could change their minds and ask for more gifts. Or they could decide that the cattle weren't fat enough or the belt not beautiful enough. More time passed, and Darlena looked nervous. Sometimes, because the gifts weren't satisfactory, a wedding was called off. But then, at long last, the bride's parents and few other members of her family entered the hogan. That was a sign that the gifts had been accepted. The delay, as it eventually turned out, was just a misunderstanding about the time of the wedding.

Then the bride entered, a beautiful, dark-haired young woman dressed in a white silk skirt and a green velveteen blouse. Watching her walk in, I caught my breath. "That could have been me," I thought. Darlena, her mother-in-law-to-be, was wearing the same green color. The groom, Erik, was wearing white jeans and a green veleveteen shirt. There was a flurry of confusion, because he'd forgotten his traditional headband. My old aunt Daisy found a pink scarf that he could roll up and use instead.

The bride carried a wedding basket, round and woven with painted circles of red, black, yellow, and natural straw. The circles were not completely closed; each left a small opening to the east for the going and coming of the spirit. The whorls that shaped the basket were a reminder that the people had come up from the center of the earth and then walked around in a widening spiral, checking out their new world. The basket was filled with a mush made of blue corn, with a design of corn pollen sprinkled on top. The bride placed the wedding basket on the ground, in front of my father. He took some of the corn pollen and then, starting at the doorway of the hogan, he sprinkled the pollen in a sacred circle.

The bride had a small pitcher of water, and she poured some into the groom's hand. In turn, he took that handful of water and poured some into her hand. Then, dipping their fingers into the wedding basket, they each took some of the corn mixture, and they fed each other with it, like Anglo brides and grooms feeding one another with wedding cake. After that, the basket was passed to the parents and close relatives, and each of us also took some of the blue corn mush.

For me, the blue corn was the taste of what might have been. "If things had been different," I kept thinking, "that might have been me." I was unsentimental, not a woman who cried at weddings, but I came close that day.

My father chanted some prayers, asking the Holy People to bless this young couple. One after another, other people rose to say a few words in Navajo. Lora translated for me. "They're giving advice," she explained. "They're telling the bride and groom to take care of each other, to respect each other, to work together, things like that." I looked at Darlena, and I could see that her eyes were misty. In the Navajo tradition, this was her son's farewell to her. In a matriarchal society, he was now supposed to go to live with his wife's family. These days, that tradition was fading, and young couples tended to live wherever it suited them. But one thing was still a strict rule. When her son's children were born, they would owe some respect to his family, but they would belong to the wife's clan.

We filed outside for a feast that the bride's family had prepared, and then a reception. Now the bride received her own gifts. In a Navajo version of the bridal registry at Bloomingdale's, a list had been made of the useful, practical things that the young couple would need to set up housekeeping—brooms and mops, pots and pans, dishes and flatware, linens, and so on. Each person chose the item he or she could afford. My gift was a bathroom set. Katie gave beautiful dishes and silverware. Three other people chipped in for a TV.

The wedding had lasted for some eight hours, and I was about ready to head home. "No, no, not yet," Darlena told me. "Come back to the hogan." Once again, just the groom's family was seated there. Then the bride's family arrived with big boxes, placing one in each person's lap. I peeked inside and saw practical, everyday staples like lard, Crisco, soda, and flour. Other members of her family came in with trays of leftovers from the feast and more bags of flour. "That's how we do it," Darlena explained. "It's up to the bride's family to send the groom's family home with food."

On the drive back from Flagstaff to Tolani, my head was full of memories. I flashed back in time to my own wedding to Dickie, so different from this one, so unplanned and unexpected.

The groom wore jeans, not white ones, just faded blue. The bride wore jeans to match. It was a surprise wedding. A surprise to the bride, that is.

We were an odd couple, the hard-scrabble Mainiac and

the Jewish princess. It was not a storybook romance, and not a match that either of our families might have planned. It was a long road, winding and bumpy, from Neponsit to Palmyra, and the two of us might never have met if other events hadn't happened first.

When stepmother Blanche packed me off to Israel, I spent two unforgettable years there. I came back mourning the death of the kibbutznik I loved, the man I wanted to marry. Yossi, darling dark-haired Yossi. He was killed in the Yom Kippur War, and I was wounded myself, with bits of shrapnel that remain in my leg to this day, setting off airport alarms. I was a wreck, but I was still unwelcome at the big white house in Neponsit.

And clever Blanche had a new idea about that. "You'd look good in blue," she told me. Before I knew it, like a one-woman family council, she had again decided my fate, and I was enlisted in the Navy. I agreed. I wanted to be gone. I did look good in blue and, for a time, my shipmates became the substitute family I was always looking for. I was in the Navy when I made my bad marriage and gave birth to Brad. Then I was out of it, because regulations didn't allow women with children. Two years later, when the regulations changed, I was back in the Navy again and stationed in New Brunswick, Maine.

I was raising Brad, then going on three, and also looking after two foster children, a troubled sister and brother from a terrible home. One night, a skinny stranger came to my door, with my foster daughter in tow. That was Dickie. He was a drinking man back then, but he worried about a teenage girl cadging drinks from strangers, and he brought her home.

He came back again and again. I was in my mid-twenties and he was fifteen years older, turning forty, a divorced father of six. But there was something shy and boyish about him, and something that reminded me of Larry Silverman.

Larry could fix anything, and so could Dickie. He did carpentry and electrical work; he was a sometime farmer and one of the first scallop divers in Maine. His wry humor made me smile. I liked the loving way he had with his children, and the patience he had with my restless, hyperactive Brad. My son tagged after him. "Can I come too?" Brad would ask whenever Dickie headed off on an errand, a visit to a friend, or a quick trip to a neighboring town, and Dickie usually said yes.

Dickie and I began as friends, and for a long time there was nothing else between us. When one of his teenage daughters had a fight with her mother, a woman who shared Dickie's drinking problem, I told her she could stay with me. Before long, another of his children came to live with me, and the others were constant visitors.

Eighteen years ago, when I first met Dickie's children, they ranged in age from three to nineteen. Growing up with two parents who were often drunk, they were used to running wild, fending for themselves, and living with more disorder than discipline. Under my roof, though, there were rules. I became the first person to say no to them, to set bedtimes for them and to ground them for breaking a rule. They balked at first, finding it strange, but they soon took it as a sign that I really cared about them.

Soon after, following in his children's footsteps, Dickie himself moved into a room in my rambling house, but we were still just friends. He was there, a part of my life, and as the song goes, I became accustomed to his face. He was stubborn and brimming with strong opinions, but he was also fiercely protective. For the first time since Bea had died and Larry had turned away from me, I had someone who made me feel safe. No one could say a cross word to me without having to deal with Dickie. Nothing could harm me as long as he was there.

We were always together but, with young children to

take care of, we never went out together. Then one night, his older children pushed us out the door. "We'll babysit," they insisted, and Dickie and I drove off for our first real date. We went to a movie, and he held my hand. Then we went parking and, like born-again teenagers, we fumbled, we groped, we got carried away in the backseat of his car.

I was nervous the next morning, and Dickie wasn't sure how to act. He put his arm around me, and I slid away from it. We went back to being friends, and to teasing one another. "If I asked you to marry me, would you?" he asked, a silly grin on his face. "Oh, sure." I laughed. "Just let me know when." He had stopped drinking, and that made him even more attractive. He kept asking and I kept laughing. Except for that one night in the car, there was nothing romantic beween us, and I was sure he was just joking.

One day, he picked me up after my shift at the naval base. "Hey," he said. "Remember all those times I asked if you'd marry me?"

"Yeah," I said, starting to laugh. "Sure."

"What if I asked you to marry me today? How about it?"

"Oh, yeah, sure," I said, still laughing.

We stopped at the house. "Wait here," he told me. He rounded up four of his older children and my young Brad, and they piled into the car with us. Brad said, "Mommy, you're getting married." I said, "Oh, yeah, sure I am."

We drove across the bridge to Orr's Island, a pretty spot on the coastline of Maine, and stopped in front of a house with a sign that said "Justice of the Peace." I still thought it was a joke, but Dickie told me that he'd been here a few days earlier, filling out the license and arranging for the paperwork to be processed. All I needed to do now was sign on the dotted line.

I was still waiting for the punchline, but the female justice of the peace seemed so pleased at her part in pulling this off. "Are you surprised?" she kept asking. "Really surprised?" She looked at me in my wedding outfit, blue jeans, blue shirt and ball cap. She grinned, delighted by the bushwhacked bride.

"Do you take this man . . ."

I started to laugh. "I don't know," I said. Dickie looked at me and then I said, "Yes, okay, I guess I will."

And so we were married. We couldn't have been more different, but somehow it worked. Somehow we have stayed together and stayed good friends as well as lovers.

The day after my nephew's Navajo wedding, my father came to see Dickie. They sat at the kitchen table, two strong and silent types hunched over cups of coffee. Finally, my father stood up.

"You owe me," he told Dickie. "You married my daughter." My father, who knew more English than he'd let on at first, had thought about this for a long time. It would be wrong to ask for too much. It would be insulting to his daughter to ask for too little, for less than the minimum bridal price.

"My daughter was worth two cattle," my father said.

My husband grinned. "Yep," he said. For the moment, we were broke, but one day, he would pay up.

CHAPTER 7

Each morning, I stepped out the door of Katie's house and, like the opening in an old hogan, it left me facing east. Looking out across the flat stretches to the distant mesa, watching the changing colors of earth and sky, I breathed in the strange beauty of the desert landscape.

"This is where I belong," I told myself. "This is home." But with each passing week, the reality of the rez was dawning on me. If this was paradise, not much grew in the garden, and there were serpents.

We had arrived empty-handed, our wallets flat. My family was sharing what they had with us but, like most Navajos, they did not have very much. Still, they put a roof over our heads. Still, they fed us on plates of mutton stew, helpings of fry bread and endless cups of strong coffee. "Don't worry," they kept saying. "We have enough." They explained something else about the Navajo way. If you have food, you're supposed to share it. If you have money, you're supposed to pass it around. If you have a lot left over, my

family told me, you need to think about it. Too many possessions are a warning. They could mean that you're doing
something wrong, that maybe you're not looking after your
relatives like you should.

I couldn't help wondering, though, how long it would
be before my family grew tired of us. We needed to find a
place of our own. We needed to start giving something back.
I'd grown up hearing children taunt one another as "an
Indian-giver," but now my family told me the true meaning
of that term. It's not someone who gives a gift and then
takes it back. It's just the reverse. It's someone who accepts
a gift and then, sometime later, maybe days, maybe months,
maybe years later, gives back something else, something different but something of value.

We had come to a place where life was hard. Over and
over, I read the tribal statistics. A majority of Navajos lived
below the poverty level. Salaries were low and prices were
high. The average annual income for a family of four, the
size of my own family, was $11,885—when you could earn
it.

Jobs were scarcer than rainfall in this place. Navajos are
famous for being industrious and hard-working, but unemployment was a fact of their life, running from a third of all
adult Navajos to a half, depending on the season. Elsewhere
on the rez, they'd found some oil, some coal and other minerals, bringing work for the people who lived there, but
bringing protests too. Strip mining scarred the landscape,
sometimes at sites that were sacred, and traditionalists saw
it as one more painful example of the white man's greed
and disrespect for Mother Earth. Our own section of the
reservation had no underground riches to tempt "the dominant culture," as they called it. My family had land, acres
of it, but it was too dry, too exhausted to yield much of a
crop or to support the big herds of cattle and sheep that

had once been the way of life and the measure of a Navajo's wealth.

I scoured the newspapers, but there were few help-wanted ads. I went to that public phone booth and dropped in endless quarters, calling every place I could think of. Finally, after weeks of searching, I found a minimum-wage job as a clerk at the hardware and home improvement store in Winslow. Everyone said I was lucky to land that. Five days a week, I drove from Tolani to Winslow, not many other cars on the road, not much attention paid to the speed limit. It was a daily round-trip of one hundred and ten miles, an expensive drive in our gas-guzzling van. Just getting to and from work took fifty-seven dollars out of my take-home pay of a hundred and eighty-four, not much to support a family of four on.

Dickie too looked for work but found nothing, not even an odd job here or there to bring in a few dollars. Even if he'd found a job, the truth was that his health wasn't up to it. But I put my paycheck together with his small disability check, and we found a place of our own, a small house that we could afford to rent. It had, as the real-estate agents say, "location, location, location." It was on a paved road, which meant I didn't have to worry about getting stuck in the deep sand that can trap your tires on the way to or from some other houses. It was within a quick drive to Katie's house, and just a few steps from where the yellow bus would stop to pick up the girls for school in nearby Leupp.

The house was a tight fit for our family. It had a kitchen, a bath, a living room, and just one bedroom. We put our names on the waiting list for a bigger place, new subsidized housing that the tribe was building in Tolani with some HUD money. In the meantime, Heather and Lori took turns sleeping on the couch in the living room and a cot in the mom-and-dad bedroom. And so forget privacy. Forget sex.

Forget even a cozy husband-and-wife chat about anything more meaningful than the weather.

My spirits rose and fell, like a Navajo chant. I was often in a "poor me" frame of mind. Each day, I drove to Winslow and looked around. The entrance to the town was marked by a big sign announcing "Navajo Country," but I'd been told that they didn't like Indians here. They were friendly enough to me in the hardware store, but on the streets, I saw for myself the mean looks on some white faces and the not-so-accidental bumps into Navajos who were just passing by.

It was a sad town, and lost people—Native Americans, whites, and Mexicans—walked up and down its streets. In the glare of high noon, there were people who were already drunk and staggering around, and other people who were stumbling along, glassy-eyed on drugs. There were old men and women who dressed in rags and slept in doorways. It hurt my heart, and it scared me. How did a person end up this way? I was just a paycheck, just a family handout, away from it. One day, one of these years, could it happen to me?

And then, one terrible day, there were the killings. "Have you heard?" they asked when I arrived at the hardware store. Four Indian men had been found murdered, beaten to death. "Young men," they told me, "in their early twenties." A chill ran through me. "It's terrible," they said, "just terrible." The bodies had been tossed in a trash Dumpster that stood right behind the police station.

I shuddered, trying to take it in. I could feel the blood draining from my face. "Are you all right, Yvette?" they asked. One of the names was familiar; one of the murdered men was my cousin, my Aunt Daisy's son. I drove home to Tolani to find my family crying. I drove back to Winslow to pick up the lumber and nails for a coffin box. I needn't have hurried. The police held on to the body, "the evidence," for three long weeks.

"Oh, dear God," I kept thinking. My family was grief-stricken, but they were strangely resigned and accepting. "The police won't do anything about it," Katie said with a deep sigh. My niece Tina nodded. "If they were whites, the police would find who did it. Even if they were Mexicans," she said. "But they were just Navajos." My family thought it was a gang killing, maybe a white gang, maybe a Mexican one. It had to be more than just one person who beat those four boys to death and then threw their bodies away, like so much trash.

The police said there were no clues, no leads. But someone must know something. Someone must have seen. Someone must have heard the scuffle, the struggle, the cries, or later heard a gang member bragging after a few drinks in a bar.

Dickie was red with anger. "We've got to do something," he kept muttering. He paced up and down, back and forth. The grieving family looked to Pete, the eldest brother, sitting there silent and stolid in his tan tribal police uniform. He too was angry. So was Katie's son, Donald, in training at the Navajo Police Academy. But there was nothing they could do. Winslow was outside the reservation, and they had no jurisdiction there. "There has to be some justice," Dickie insisted. In Maine, he had lived by an ethos. "If a man hurts me or one of mine, I'll hurt him back," he used to tell me. "And he'll know it was me who did it."

He was in a fury. He couldn't accept that the Winslow police would do nothing about this. But my family had seen it before. They knew that Navajo lives were held cheap. It was one more pain to add to their deep grief. With a terrible calm, they waited for the police to release the body. Then they held the death ceremony, a two-day chantway.

They carried the body to the little church in Tolani, a building that stood empty most of the time, used only for funerals and for the summer programs run by different

Christian organizations. Not many people in Tolani followed the Jesus road, but the missionaries still came every summer, always hopeful.

There, in that half-abandoned church, a medicine man chanted the traditional prayers, trying to explain why this had happened. He told the ancient story of how Death, one of the great monsters that the Twin Heroes had not managed to slay, became a part of our world and our lives. Traditionally, Navajos had buried their dead above the ground, arranging the body so that it faced east, then covering it with a cairn of stones. But agents from the BIA (Bureau of Indian Affairs) had put a stop to that, claiming that it was "unsanitary," and there was no longer an Indian burial ground in Tolani. Instead, the body was taken to a cemetery in Winslow, the same cemetery where my mother was buried.

All through this, Dickie kept after me, wanting me to quit my job. I reminded him of how hard it had been to find this job, how hard it would be to replace and how much we needed the paycheck. But Dickie was worried about my working in Winslow. Even before the killings, it was known as a dangerous place for Indians. Day or night, man or woman, you could get jumped there.

The thought of it scared me. It wasn't so much a fear of being attacked, but I was frightened of my own feelings and my own anger. I was afraid of losing control and hitting back in a blind fury. Once again, I might do something that I regretted.

Because in another life, in a very different place, it had happened before. . . .

Israel was a world away from Tolani. In the northern Galilee, where I lived on a collective farm called Kibbutz Sa'ar, it was rolling hills, green fields, and orchards ripe with oranges and avocados and bananas. I came there as a stranger, "a spoiled American," as they called me before they knew me, but I wanted to belong to this place and these people.

God appeared to Abraham and gave this land to him and his posterity. I grew up believing that I was his descendant, his heir to the land of Israel. I was there now, groping for words, stammering in a strange tongue, the language of the Bible. In this place, I worked with my hands for the first time. It felt like a place I could call home, a promised land where I could find a new family.

Everyone here was connected, like a Navajo clan. There were 350 people at Kibbutz Sa'ar, and that meant I had that many mothers and fathers, aunts and uncles, sisters and brothers. "Everyone has something to contribute," they told me. "Everyone has a place here." I came with no practical skills, a girl who grew up taking piano lessons and dance classes, but they had new lessons to teach me—a new language, a new way of life, a new pride in ordinary work. I worked side by side with them, an awkward girl peeling her first potatoes in the kitchen, bleeding on them when her knife slipped. I climbed tall ladders with them, picking the fruit that grew high on the trees. I tended the dairy herd, milking the cows, nursing the young calves, even helping with the miracle of their birth. For the first time since Bea's death, I felt like someone who was wanted, someone who belonged.

I was seventeen and living in a communal coed dorm, sharing a room with two sun-dark *sabras*, native-born Israelis, named after the cactus fruit that's tough on the outside, sweet on the inside. That's what Yossi and his brother Yuda were like. Their parents had built a nation, and now they would defend it. "You too, Yvette," Yossi said. "You're an Israeli now." I had "made *aliyah*," as the Israelis call it when a Jew returns to live in the Promised Land, and I was now a citizen.

We were close to the Lebanon border, and tension was

building again between Arabs and Israelis. They showed me how to use an Uzi, and I carried that gun when we went on night patrol. The kibbutzniks who were army veterans walked the outer perimeter, and we younger ones walked the inner one. We couldn't see the enemy, but we could hear sniper fire. Now and then, a grenade landed close by, in the banana fields. We'd call out to one another in the darkness, counting heads. "Is everyone okay?" No one was ever hurt, and I felt like someone playing at war. I never dreamed that I would fire that gun at a living target.

Yossi and I began as friends, almost as kibbutz brother and sister. He was sweet and funny, and we were partners in mischief. One night, we crept into the hen coop, stole a chicken, and raced to the edge of the kibbutz for an illicit cookout. But as the months passed, I began to feel something else.

More and more, I was drawn to Yossi. He was six feet tall, slim and strong, a mop of dark curls on his head, a sun-bronzed idealist in a blue kibbutz shirt. One night, walking back from patrol, he kissed me, and it went to my head like Galilee wine. We kissed again the next night and the next. He became the first man I ever petted with, the first man I ever talked about marriage with. I was going on eighteen, a dropout from the sexual revolution, still a virgin. We agreed that sex could wait until our wedding night.

But the talk of war was becoming louder. The tension was building. When I turned eighteen, I went into the army, like any other Israeli, and was taking my training at a base near Haifa. Many of my kibbutz friends were in the same group of new recruits.

Late one night, four of us walked along the dark, almost deserted streets of Haifa. Three of us were unarmed and dressed in kibbutz dungarees, but the fourth, Rafael, was handsome in his uniform, his army beret tilted at a jaunty angle, his Uzi slung over his shoulder. He was returning to a base in another part of Israel, and we were walking him to the bus station. We were passing a graveyard. "Whistle," I told them, explaining the American custom for keeping ghosts at bay. We were laughing and joking, not paying much attention.

We barely noticed the Arab who was walking toward us. He began to walk faster, and then he was running toward us. It happened without warning. Suddenly, he was upon us. At the last second, I caught the glint of a large knife in his hand. But it was too late. The Arab lunged at Rafael, and in one terrible stroke, he slashed at his stomach, gutting him.

The rest was in slow motion. I saw the world in red, the dark red color of the blood that was spilling from my friend. As Rafael was going down, I grabbed for his Uzi. I pointed the gun at the escaping Arab and squeezed the trigger. The explosion rang in my ears, and I fired again. The Uzi recoiled, slamming against my shoulder, and I lost count of the shots.

The Arab was hit, staggering, falling, and I ran after him. I became aware of people shouting, coming out of nearby houses and running to help us. The Arab was down on the pavement, the bloody knife next to him. He was not moving, not making a sound, and I didn't know if he was dead or still alive. But I was out of control. I took the Arab's knife and stabbed him with it. I was mad with grief. I was crazy with anger. I stabbed him again. I couldn't stop stabbing him.

The police arrived and my friends pulled me away from the Arab's body. I was trembling. "Come away, Yvette," they said. Their faces were ashen and streaked with tears. "Rafael?" I asked, and they shook their heads. We stood there a moment, hugging one another, unable to speak, and I could feel their shoulders shaking with sobs.

I was covered with Rafael's blood and the Arab's; I

didn't know which red stain was which. I couldn't stop crying. For Rafael. And for the Arab. My friends told me that I'd acted like a soldier. "*Tov*, Yvette," they said. "You did well, Yvette." But I couldn't stop shaking. "I killed him," I kept thinking. "I killed that man."

For weeks afterward, I was red-eyed and sleepless. Night after night, I woke from the same nightmare. I kept seeing myself holding that knife, my hands covered in blood as I stabbed that man again and again. I had killed the man who killed my friend, but I had kept stabbing him even after he was dead. I had that nightmare for many years, and it made me afraid of my own anger. It was an emotion that lived like a *dybbuk* within me, and I had to be careful not to let it out. "This is what can happen when you get angry," I warned myself. "You can kill someone."

Yossi held me in his arms. He didn't understand. He too thought I'd acted like a good soldier. But his love helped me through it. Finally, we stopped talking about it and started to plan our future together. I wanted to live in Israel forever. I wanted to stay in his arms forever. We promised to love one another forever.

We had a kibbutz wedding, no caterer, no rented hall, no fancy clothes. For the outdoor ceremony, I wore my kibbutz uniform, dungarees and a blue shirt, boots, and a work hat. Yossi was in his army uniform. Side by side, surrounded by our kibbutz family, we stood under a wedding canopy and said our vows in front of the rabbi. "Behold," I said, pledging love in a loud voice, wanting everyone to hear, "you are consecrated unto me as my husband . . ." Then Yossi stepped on the glass, breaking it with a loud pop, in memory of the destruction of the Temple, the sadness that Jews are supposed to recall even in the middle of great joy. And then Yossi kissed me.

We were married in the eyes of God, but we weren't legally marrried, not yet. We'd rushed the ceremony because war was imminent, but there was still paperwork to deal with and forms I needed to sign at the American Embassy, because I had dual citizenship. We agreed that we'd wait for a couple of days, until we could make everything legal, and then we'd consummate our marriage.

We never had the chance to do that. The next day was Saturday, October 6, 1973. Without warning, the armies of Syria and Egypt invaded our small country, and the Yom Kippur War began. Yossi and I, Yuda and the rest of our group, raced to Haifa to get our orders. Then we retraced our steps, sent to a base not far from Kibbutz Sa'ar and assigned to patrol and protect the coastline from that area to the Lebanese border.

Most of the fighting was along the Egyptian and Syrian borders, but we never knew when an army might come storming across the border from Lebanon. Every day, we went out to patrol the shoreline. We were looking for lone infiltrators or small advance cadres. We explored the caves at Rosh Haniquere, small grottos formed by the endless waves of the Mediterranean, big enough places for an enemy to hide. We took some sniper fire. We took some grenades. But the shooting was random, meant to harass and intimidate, not yet an all-out attack.

We were patrolling north of Rosh Haniquere, very close to the border, when the barrage began. Suddenly, the world exploded. They were firing mortars and land missiles at us. There was the steady *pop-pop-pop* of rifle fire. There was the wind and great heat of a pineapple grenade and the smell of sulfur as it exploded next to me. My heart was pounding, but all I felt was a quick sting, a flashback to childhood and the time I scraped my hands and knees on some gravel.

They caught us in an open area, with only a scattering of rocks and some trees. I took cover behind one of the rocks, and I could see Yossi just two or three feet away, hugging the ground. The noise was deafening. The explosions were blinding. It seemed to go on forever. When I looked again, I could no longer see Yossi. People were calling to one another. "Are you okay?" I began to call out too. "Yossi," I yelled. "Yossi, are you okay?" There was no answer. There was a leg blown apart from its body. There were pieces of bodies, bloody pieces of my friends, everywhere.

"Everybody out!" came the order. "Everybody out of here!" I started running, scrambling over rocks, moving fast out of the killing field. I was running hard when I heard someone shouting at me. "Stop," he yelled. "You're hit." I shook my head. I didn't think I'd been hit. But someone grabbed me. Someone bandaged me and put me on a litter in the back of a truck headed for the hospital in Nahariya.

When I woke in the hospital, there were burns all over my body, and bits of shrapnel from that pineapple grenade. A bullet that I never even felt had plowed across my back. It was a disaster for our unit. Yossi was dead. So were too many others. Yuda was still alive, lying on a bed down the hallway, his left foot gone.

I felt a terrible emptiness. One minute my friends were there, and the next minute they were gone, blown apart. I felt an aching guilt. Why Yossi? I was just two feet away from him. Why my sweet bridegroom? Why not me?

I was in the hospital for about a month, while they removed as much of the shrapnel as they could. During that time, a half-forgotten voice called me on the phone, my adoptive father, Larry Silverman. The hospital had notified him that I'd been wounded. "Come home, Yvette," he said. I explained that Israel was now my home. "Come back, Yvette," he said. "At least for a while. At least until you're all well." Then he made a promise to me. "Later, if you want to go back to Israel, I'll buy you the ticket."

I flew back to America, still thinking of Israel as my home, still planning to return there. But I never have returned. I used to tell myself that it was because Larry broke his promise to give me the plane ticket, and I didn't have the money to buy one myself.

But I have figured out at least one thing during my on-and-off Vision Quest. Maybe, with Yossi dead, that was just an excuse. Or maybe, as the Navajos would say, the Holy People had other plans for me—a different place for me to go and a different family for me to find.

I never got to say good-bye to Yossi. I never had the chance to say good-bye to the people at Kibbutz Sa'ar. I would have liked to have done that. *"Shalom,* Yossi," I wanted to say. "Peace, my darling. Peace, my friends."

Each night, in that crowded little bedroom in Tolani, I still said the *Shema Yisroel.* I prayed for peace and I asked for harmony. "C'mon, God," I whispered, "make this work."

CHAPTER 8

"Too much death," my sister Katie said, her dark eyes looking large and worried behind her glasses. My Navajo family did not approve of the life I had led as a Lost Bird. They listened to my stories of Israel. They heard about the other events of my past, and they were afraid for me.

"Too much blood," my Aunt Despah said, her face turning pale. My history was crowded with episodes that were dangerous and, for a Navajo woman, taboo.

I had seen war and death in Israel. It left me with terrible dreams and I still woke sometimes, half a world away, with that old nightmare. My family nodded and looked anxious at that. In the Navajo way of looking at the world, I would never find *hozho*, or harmony, until I had dealt with the demons of my past. As my family explained, it was dangerous to be present at death, and especially at the death of an enemy. As they saw it, I could still be haunted by that long-ago Arab's *chindi*, the evil spirit or ghost that lingered after any person's death. Wanting revenge, it could have followed me to this distant desert.

"You need a ceremony," Aunt Despah told me. "You need it soon." Life on the rez moved to the rhythm of Blessing Ways and Enemy Ways, Crystal Gazings and Hand Tremblings. My aunt talked of a cleansing ceremony to wash away the taint. She spoke of a four-day ghost ceremony such as the one both of us had just attended for a clan relative.

For three days, they had chanted and burned cedar and sage within the ceremonial hogan. When dawn came up on the fourth day, the man had emerged from the hogan, his body blackened with ashes, a disguise to baffle any lurking, vengeful *chindi*. His wife walked behind him, sweeping away his footsteps so that no *chindi* could follow after him. It was ritual playacting, dreamlike and very powerful.

"You need a ceremony," my Aunt Despah said again, and I nodded. I yearned to exorcize the ghosts that had followed me from Neponsit, from Israel, from everywhere. I wanted to mend body and spirit, and I was beginning to believe in ceremonies and chantways, and in the healing therapy of words and drumbeats, prayer sticks and ashes, cedar smoke and eagle feathers.

As my family listened to my history, they heard of other things that needed exorcizing. Over the years, I'd worked as an EMT, an Emergency Medical Technician, on ambulances and in emergency rooms. I'd helped to save some people, but I'd also been present at moments of death, moments when a *chindi* is released. The Navajos believe that even a good person has this speck of evil, this *chindi*, that is released at death and left behind when the person returns to Father Sun. The tradition is so powerful that some people still refuse to go on living in a hogan or a house where someone has died. Even after the death of a beloved family member, they may seal up the doors and windows and move away. Sometimes, not wanting to abandon a family home, they may carry the dying person outside, to release the *chindi* under the open sky.

At times, I'd also worked as a nursing assistant in hospitals and old-age homes. I'd eased the pain of the sick and I'd held the hands of the dying, comforting them in their last moments. I was proud of that work, but over the years, I'd been there at the deathbeds of as many as a hundred people. "White people," my family pointed out nervously. I tried to shut my ears to those bits and pieces of prejudice but, for some Navajos, white people were still "the enemy," and that made their *chindi* even more malevolent. I had been present at the death of too many of them, multiplying my risk of illnesses that can't be explained, physical ailments and mental disturbances that they call "corpse sickness."

In my past, there was still more to worry my family. At times, I'd gone hunting with Dickie, a forbidden activity for a Navajo woman. "Yvette's a crack shot," Dickie bragged to them. "She never misses." My family shuddered at that. As they warned me, animals too have *chindi*. By tradition, Navajo wives do not hunt, lest the animal's *chindi* follow them home and harm their children. By custom, even Navajo husbands do not go hunting when their wives are pregnant or their children are very young, relying instead on tribal relatives to provide the meat they may need. One of my nieces believes that her little child has become ill, with a serious intestinal malady, because her husband went hunting too soon after the child's birth.

My sister Katie kept after me. "We need to have a ceremony for you," she said again and again. There were Hand Trembler ceremonies in which a medicine man passed fluttering hands over the patient's body to diagnose a problem and prescribe a remedy—perhaps a visit to a white doctor, perhaps another ceremony. Sometimes the Hand Trembler seems to be able to do this just by touching a piece of clothing. One Tolani woman, feeling poorly, sent her shirt to a Hand Trembler. Sensing something very wrong, the Hand Trembler clutched at his stomach. Told about this, the woman raced to the hospital, arriving just in time to be saved from a burst appendix.

There were also searching ceremonies, such as the ones my father had done over the years to look for his missing twins. And there were the longer ceremonies, the chantways that could last for days. By now, I had seen the peace that those chantways can bring, and I had heard the beauty and the promise of their words:

Heya neya yana,
I have come upon it, I have come upon blessing.
People, my relatives, I have come upon blessing. . . .

But I hesitated. The chantway that I seemed to need was lengthy, elaborate, and expensive. The blessing would be stronger if my entire clan family, perhaps two hundred people, were there. Gifts were often called for. Food would be needed. Something had to be given in exchange for a blessing, and so the hataali, even if he was my father, would have to be paid. For now, I didn't have the money. My sisters offered to chip in and pay for everything, but it was hard for me to keep taking and taking. Navajos live, think, and act as a community, but I still had a lingering white-world longing to be self-sufficient.

"I want to pay my own way," I tried to explain.

"Okay," my sister said. "But don't wait too long, Yvette. Don't wait too long."

Meanwhile, I listened to the stories of Tolani Lake. There were ghosts on the reservation, the chindi of the departed. And witches, people who used the ancient ceremonies for evil rather than good. And skinwalkers, people who were like Navajo werewolves, turning from human into night-stalking animals and back again. My family kept warning me about them. It was not just my white-world past that made me vulnerable. As a twin, believed to be born with special powers, I was also a prime target of this malevolence. A witch might envy my supposed power, or be afraid of it, or want to steal some of it, and then try to conjure up some harm to me.

At night, over cups of coffee, my family told endless stories. Many years ago, the family hogan had caught on fire, and my sister Lora had been trapped inside. She was just three years old, one of the twins born after my brother and I went missing, and she was burned over half of her body. Lora spent long years in the hospital, having skin grafts, undergoing one operation after another. She emerged shy and self-conscious about the scars that she hid under long sleeves and flowing skirts. She was painfully with-drawn until the wonderful Sam Chee came along, galloping over the sand dunes and telling her it didn't matter.

For my family, the fire was not simply a terrible acci-dent. They believed that a witch, jealous of Lora's power as a twin, had caused the fire. In a small community, they could figure out who it was, and knowing the witch's name gave them the power to turn the evil back on her. Navajos believed that the scales were always balanced and, a year or so later, the witch herself was trapped in a fire.

I shivered at that story. As they grew up, Lora and her twin sister Louva were kept apart, one of them at home, the other with a relative, to hide their twinship from other witches. My family also was convinced that some witches, envious and resentful of the power of twins, had performed black magic over the years to block the search for me and my brother. I was a neo-Navajo, not yet sure what to believe, or how much, but I did know one thing: jealousy can be very bad medicine.

As the weeks passed, I could see for myself that I was being followed and haunted. From the window of my little rented house, I could see an old woman coming closer and closer. She was small and hunchbacked, with gnarled, restless hands. Day after day, she was there, mumbling to herself and staring at my house. When she thought no one was looking, she would circle the house three times, muttering and mumbling. Her long skirts were dusty from the six miles she'd walked from her desert home to mine, and dotted with thistles from the scrub bushes she'd brushed against. My family knew all about her, and they told me that she was evil on the hoof.

Hidden behind a curtain, I watched as the old woman hobbled closer. That morning, she stopped in the front yard, looking around, as if to reassure herself that no one was watching. She failed to spot me and she came still closer. I saw her bending down, slowly, creakily, until she was kneeling at the doorstep. With unsteady hands, she pulled out a paper bag and filled it with sand. And then, after another quick look around, she left.

I was puzzled. Later, I told it to Katie as a foolish story. "There's sand everywhere," I said. "Why would that old woman want some of mine?" Instead of laughing with me, Katie looked alarmed. The hunchback had taken something that belonged to me, something she needed to work her evil spell. "Yvette, be very careful," my sister warned. "Everyone knows that woman is a witch."

Navajos are on constant guard against the supernatural. Even when they're not being stalked by a witch, they make it a daily habit to burn the stray hairs that might get caught in a brush or comb, and to do the same with fingernail clippings. When they throw away a letter with their name on it, some Navajos tear it first into small pieces, lest it fall into the wrong hands. My family told me to be especially wary. The old woman had taken what she could get, but her spell would be even stronger if she had something more intimate than sand.

A few nights later, hidden by the darkness, the old woman returned. The next morning, I opened the front door and found a bloody package. I knew who had left it and, when I poked it open with a stick, I felt sick. The grisly package held the afterbirth of an animal, probably a sheep. I shuddered. In disgust, I dug a hole and buried it. I was shaking with anger at the bloody token that had been left like a curse on my doorstep. My sisters were more alarmed than ever and my young daughters, hearing the stories, were beginning to be afraid.

When the old woman appeared again, I confronted her. She flinched when she saw me coming through the front door. She flinched again when I pointed a finger at her, a Navajo gesture of contempt. We stood under the hot Arizona sun, facing one another in the sandy yard. She spoke no English, and I knew little Navajo. I accused her in sign language, and she understood every angry gesture.

Pointing to the doorstep and then to her, I accused her of having left that bloody package. She took a step back, shaking her head from side to side in denial. I glared at her, nodding my head up and down to say yes. I pointed two fingers at my eyes, then pointed again to her, a gesture that said, "I saw you do it." When she kept shaking her head, I used one finger to draw a circle around my mouth, sign language that said, "You're lying." I bent to pick up some sand, to tell her that I knew about that as well.

Then I brushed my hands against each other, an angry gesture that said, "That's enough!" The old woman seemed to shrink in fear. She believed in the power that twins are said to have, and the grim look on my face was a warning that made her tremble. She took a few steps backward, then she turned and hurried away.

After that day, the old woman stopped haunting my house. Then, as time passed, I heard that she was having serious health problems. I had not wished her any harm, but I had named and confronted her. Maybe she believed that, by doing that, I had turned the evil back on her. Maybe her own black thoughts were making her sick.

The reservation sat in a place where the earth had once cracked open, heaving up mountains and carving out canyons. Centuries of wind had shaped the high mesas and sculpted the sandstone buttes. Tolani Lake sat on one of the vast stretches of flat desert, a scattering of houses surrounded by an immense silence. It was a landscape where astronauts once practiced for their lunar landings. It was a territory with no borders between the dream world and the real one.

My little rented house sat atop a slight rise in the landscape. The new house that I was hoping for was still taking shape, still just an empty shell sitting among the grid of new buildings that were going up at the other end of Tolani. Some twenty new homes were being built, and I was on the waiting list for one of them.

"C'mon, God," I prayed. "At least another bedroom." It was March, my promised moving date, but something had gone wrong. There was a delay. Then it was May, another promised move-in date, but there were more and more problems at the building site.

Night after night, from my little hilltop, I could hear the dogs barking at the building site. People told me that they tried to quiet them, but the dogs seemed crazed. They would not stop their barking and frantic howling, almost as if the dogs had sniffed some danger or heard some warning that was out of human range.

From the day that the first spade of earth was turned on that site, there had been an odd series of troubles. A workman was badly hurt. And then another. The concrete that was delivered was the wrong mix. Walls were put up, only to fall down for no apparent reason. The electricity went haywire. A foundation cracked. The plumbing wouldn't work. Still another workman was hurt. Each event could be explained, but the number of unlucky events had people whispering about an evil spell on that building project.

As the houses were completed, one by one, people moved in, and tragedy seemed to follow those new tenants. Many of them had come from far out beyond the dunes. They'd been living in isolated hogans. Now they were living with electricity, with indoor plumbing, and with the unfamiliar closeness of neighbors. It was a leap into the twentieth century, and some of them found it stressful. Some began to drink too much. Others began to abuse their children or their wives. For the first time, the teenagers found themselves in a cluster of other teens, and they formed a gang, racing headlong into trouble. Progress had its price, and some of the new people had bad dreams. They wondered if it was something from the past, something that was haunting them by day as well as by night.

Death too seemed to follow them. Two people were run over by cars. Someone was found in the sand dunes, dead of heatstroke. A young child died suddenly. Someone else committed suicide. A mother wept over a baby who was born dead. There was a reasonable explanation for each death, but in this tiny collection of houses, within the space of a few months, there were more deaths than seemed normal.

The people of Tolani grew anxious and fearful, and maybe that's why the trouble spread beyond the housing site. Once-loving couples began to argue. Careful drivers began to have accidents. There was a rise in drunkenness, a rise in arrests, a rise in domestic violence. I heard screams in the night from wives who'd never been beaten before. Social workers talked of the poverty, the unemployment, the tensions that were disrupting so many Navajo families. Each problem had a rational cause, but the coincidences mounted in an irrational way.

Tolani responded in the Navajo way. They called in the medicine men, and my father was one of several who came from different areas. They did ceremonies to search for the cause of the problem, and each came to the same conclusion. The houses were being built on the site of an old graveyard. The excavations had disturbed the dead and aroused their *chindi*.

Even the eldest people in Tolani could not remember a graveyard on that site. But when the Chapter House dug through the old records, they found a note about a centuries-old graveyard. At that point, the builders finally admitted that, when the site was first excavated, they had indeed found some bones. Rather than delay the construction, they'd decided to say nothing about it.

Now the medicine men performed other ceremonies, to calm the *chindi* at the housing site. Some of the people had individual ceremonies done, to exorcise their bad dreams. Peace returned to Tolani. The *chindi* were the Navajo way of explaining evil and misfortune. Maybe they were real. Maybe they were a scapegoat, something to blame for evil that was beyond human understanding, something to pin the troubles on and then chase off into the desert.

Real or not, the *chindi* were gone. The building began again, and I waited, not very patiently, for a new move-in date. "Maybe September," I was told.

There were ghosts in the white world too. I grew up knowing how to ward off bad luck. I knocked on wood. I crossed my fingers and tossed salt over my shoulder. I came of age hearing about *dybbuks*, creatures who could take possession of a person, and *golems*, clay creatures who were brought to life with secret incantations, trained to obey their masters but sometimes running amok. And I knew, from personal experience, about the evil eye.

Between Israel and Maine, between Yossi and Dickie, there was Bob Simon, my best friend in all the world, the man I didn't marry. We met in Neponsit when the two of us were working on the emergency ambulance, me just back from the war in Israel, he just returned from the one in Vietnam. When it became impossible for me to live with my father Larry and my stepmother Blanche, Bob came to my rescue. He packed my bags and took me home to his mother, the wonderful Frieda Simon.

At first, she seemed unaware that I was there. I was a stranger, walking around her house like a shadow, coming and going from my job as quietly as I could. Three days passed before Frieda and I actually spoke. And then, in her kitchen, Frieda broke the silence. "And so?" she asked. "You're living here?" She opened the refrigerator. "And so?" she asked again. "Why aren't you eating?"

She never blinked. She just opened her arms and made me her daughter. Her son and I were always together, and Frieda would get a bright, hopeful look in her eyes. Bob and I were better as friends than as lovers, but now and then, we talked idly about marriage. Frieda would urge us on, dreaming of a wedding. But Bob and I were too alike, and both of us were too wounded by the wars we'd just lived through.

Instead, I left for my first brief stint in the Navy, and Frieda's house became the place I came home to on leave. Instead, I married someone else, a dark-eyed Navy officer, dysfunctional and often violent, eventually diagnosed as a paranoid schizophrenic. When it was over, I was twenty-two years old, pregnant with my first child, and homeless. Once again, Frieda opened her arms to me. "And so?" she asked. "Isn't this your home? Where else would you go?" Maybe she was still hoping that Bob and I might marry, but she clucked over me all through the pregnancy, full of advice and full of pleasure over my growing belly. She raced after me to the hospital when the time came to welcome my son Brad into the world.

The next day, she was there when Larry and Blanche came

to my hospital room. They had an attorney waiting in the corridor, along with a married couple who wanted to adopt my son. "Everything is all arranged," Larry told me. "All you have to do is sign the papers." I was too startled to speak. "It's for the best," he was saying. "Just sign the papers." I stared at him. He seemed to expect that, as always, I'd do as he told me to. "No," I managed to whisper. "No."

Frieda was right there, a woman at no loss for words. "No adoption. No way," she announced. "Yvette is coming home with me. She's my daughter. And the baby is coming with me too. He's my grandson."

Eight days after Brad was born, Frieda was bustling around her house, preparing for the guests who were coming for the *bris,* or circumcision. She had an armload of red ribbons, and she hung them all over Brad's crib. "That looks pretty," I told her. I thought it made the crib look festive. Then I watched as she hung red ribbons everywhere, on the mirrors, the pictures, the door jambs, wherever she could tack one on. I wondered what she was doing with so many red ribbons. "Frieda," I asked, "what are you up to?"

"Blanche is coming," she explained. I didn't understand. "It's to protect the baby," she said. She gave me a long, serious look. Her face set in determination, she pinned up still more red ribbons. For an orthodox Jew like Frieda, they were the traditional way to ward off bad luck for a new baby. "Blanche is coming," she said again. "We have to protect against her evil eye."

Larry saw the red ribbons, and though he didn't say anything, he knew what they were for. I stayed in Neponsit for a half a year or so, and during those months Larry often came to visit me and Brad. He'd arrive unannounced, and he'd sit there quietly, holding the baby in his arms. I saw the look of love on his face, and I remembered that, once upon a time, he'd looked at me in that same way. For a few years, with Bea to show him the way, he was a wonderful father. Then Bea died, the love of his life, and maybe he never came to terms with that loss. In his pain and confusion, maybe he forgot how to be caring and how to be loving. Maybe he too had ghosts and needed a ceremony.

I looked at my adoptive father, holding the only grandson he would ever have, and the old anger and resentment melted away, replaced by sadness and pity. Larry never stayed more than five or ten minutes. Then, with a wan smile, he'd leave. As he explained, he'd told Blanche that he was only going out to pick up a cigar, and that he'd only be gone for a little while.

As time passed, the red ribbons didn't seem to have worked. Brad was a difficult child, hyperactive, plagued with an attention deficit, learning difficulties and emotional problems. At times, I wondered if he'd inherited some imbalance from his disturbed father. I always focused on my son's moments of sweetness but, in his frustration, Brad was sometimes out of control.

Maybe, as many red ribbons as we had, they weren't enough. Blanche was not the only person who wanted to separate me from my son. When I reenlisted in the Navy, they wanted me to put Brad in a boarding school, so that I could be sent overseas. I refused. From the time he turned three, I took him to psychiatrists. They pinned labels on him: "ADD," "oppositional behavior," "behavioral impairment." They gave him pills, but no medicine seemed to work better than my own loving arms around him.

I fought endless battles with schools and social agencies, trying to get Brad the help he needed. All they ever wanted to do was put him away in a hospital or a juvenile home. I felt he was making real progress, living at home and learning how to cope. I was out of the Navy now, with more time to devote to him, and he was surrounded by a family who cared about him, my two little daughters and Dickie's older children.

Yet when Brad was fifteen, a state social agency finally had its way. They produced a statement that Brad had made when he was five years old. "I'm mad at my mother," he had told the social worker. "I'm going to kill her. And then I'm going to kill everyone else." It was the sort of thing that any frustrated little child might say in anger, but ten years later the social agency was using it as proof that Brad was a danger to the family. He was a boy who'd never shown any sign of violence toward me, toward his little sisters, toward Dickie or anyone else. Yet the social agency was now threatening to take my daughters away, "for their own safety," if Brad were not removed from the house.

No mother should have to face such a threat. I sat in a courtroom, listening to all of this, and I could feel my heart cracking. Nothing I said seemed to matter to a judge who sat stone-faced on a high bench. Armed with that judge's order, insisting that everyone would be better off that way, they took my innocent son away from me. They pushed him into a van and drove him off to a therapeutic foster home. Soon after, he ran away from that place, making his way back to my house. They tracked him down, pulled him from my arms and took him to another foster home. I visited as often as I was allowed. Before very long, though, Brad ran away from that home too, disappearing into the streets.

Almost five years have passed, but I have thought of him every day. Now and then, I have heard from him, but the last phone call was a long time ago. I have left messages everywhere, with every friend or relative he might turn to, telling him where to find me. I have gone to meetings with other mothers with children like Brad, and we've wept together over a social system that refused to give us the help we needed, preferring instead to pay strangers to look after our sad children.

These days, when I think of Brad, I think of my birth mother. She had a son stolen, and a daughter. Brad was

older when it happened, but he too was stolen. He is my
lost and wounded bird, and I want him here in Tolani. So
do Dickie and the girls. This is where he belongs. I wait for
a call, a letter, a word from him, so that I can give him
directions to this place where he can be healed.

In Tolani, I was beginning to define myself. I was white
and Jewish by upbringing, and Navajo by the powerful tug
of blood. My family talked of people who had left the reservation and become physically ill. "Heartsickness," they
called it. When Dickie grumbled and talked of leaving, I too
felt that pang. I had lived in so many places—Neponsit,
Israel, Maine and points in between. I'd been sorry to leave
some of those places and some of those people, but I'd never
looked back and felt homesick. Yet if I had to leave the
rez, there would be something crying within me. I didn't
understand why, not yet. But at just the mention of it, my
heart hurt.

It would not be easy to stay. There were problems here.
Maybe there were *chindi*, but there was also wickedness that
was human.

One morning, I opened my front door and stared at the
graffiti-covered water tower that stood not far away. During
the night, someone had added a new message. I blinked at
the hateful words.

"Kill whitey."

My heart was pounding. I thought of Dickie and my
half-white daughters, and my hands began to shake. I don't
know how long I stood there, staring at those words. When
I finally walked back through the door, Dickie caught the
look on my face. Troubled by back pains, he'd been up since
before dawn. "Yep," he said grimly. "I know. I saw it too."

My hands were still unsteady. The dishes rattled as I
put breakfast on the table. My daughters had seen something even worse than the words, and now they told us
about it. "This older boy stopped me and Lori the other

day," Heather said. "He showed us a knife. He told us he was going to use it to kill whitey." Heather admitted that it had frightened her. "But not a lot," she insisted. "I thought he was just showing off."

I listened, my face hot with anger. I didn't want to alarm the girls by making too much of it, but I realized who Heather was talking about. I'd seen him hanging around. That teenager with the knife, the same one who must have painted those words on the water tower, was related to me. He was a young man with a troubled history, just thirteen years old and a nephew of mine, two or three times removed. In the Navajo scheme of things, that still made him my clan son.

Later that day, I tracked him down. In front of his friends, I gave him a tongue-lashing. "Stay away from my family," I warned him. "Don't mess with them. Or you'll have me to deal with." He heard from his parents and other relatives too. For the people of Tolani, the big question was not racism but family respect. The boy had disrespected me, his clan mother. He had disrespected Heather and Lori, his clan sisters. He had disrespected Dickie, a white man but also his clan uncle. With that episode, the latest in his string of troubles, the community turned against him. As word of it spread, the teen was sent to live in exile—off the reservation.

But if the mischief-maker was gone, the graffiti stayed there. No one painted over the words. Dickie, the hard-boiled Mainiac, the taciturn man who hid his deepest feelings, seemed to shrug it off. Yet I wondered. As a Jew, I'd seen hateful graffiti before, but Dickie was a white Christian, full of his own prejudices and not used to being the target. "Don't take it personally," my sister Katie told him.

"Well, tell me, Katie," he said, giving her one of his looks, "how many other whiteys do you see around here?"

CHAPTER 9

In the light of early morning, in the schizophrenia of who I used to be and who I was becoming, I stood outside, still barefoot, still uncombed, still astonished at the heartbreaking beauty of sunrise over Tolani.

The *Dineh* say that the Holy People have left the earth, but that they continue to be present in the wind, or in the wings of an eagle, or in the pollen that wafts from the corn and other growing plants. They say that the Holy People come to check each house at dawn. Some Navajo mothers wake their children early and shoo them outside, hoping the Holy People will see them and bless them.

I missed those blessings as a child. Now, as a grown woman, watching the first pink blush of the morning sun turn to orange and brilliant streaks of red, I hoped it was not too late for a blessing or two. I'd learned a Navajo prayer, and I whispered it now. "May I walk happily and lightly on the earth." It was a plea for a good life that did no harm.

Day in, day out, I thought of the ancient Navajo proverb: "Walk in harmony within the universe by being aware of who you are."

For me, that was still an open question. The dawns came and went. The moon moved through its cycles. But I often felt like someone who had sprung, fully grown, from someone else's imagination. Even my name was up for grabs. For a lifetime, I'd been Yvette, but now some people were urging me to use my birth name, my Navajo name, Minnie Bob. It did not roll easily off my tongue. It sounded odd to my ears, though I answered when my Aunt Despah and some other older people called me that.

I had turned for help to the DNBA, the *Dinebeiina Nahilna Be Agaditahe*, the Navajo legal services agency, sometimes translated as "the ones who talk fast to help people." They had started the process of activating my census number, my identity in the tribe. Meanwhile, I was told that I could begin to use the census number to apply for housing, for jobs, and other help.

I needed help. Life on the rez was harder than I'd anticipated, and I was desperate to find another job, something better than the gas-guzzler I'd finally left in Winslow, something that would actually feed my family. I applied for every little job opening I heard about, but nothing materialized.

I had come here, drawn by flesh and blood, back to the place where my umbilical cord was buried. For Navajos, it's very important to know where that place is. They believe that if you don't know where your umbilical cord is buried, then you may be fated to spend all of your life searching for it. When little children go rummaging through drawers, Navajo parents laugh and say that it's the umbilical cord they're looking for. My nephew Darrell, Katie's eldest son, told me a Navajo joke about that. "People say that if you want your child to grow up rich, you should bury the umbilical cord near a bank."

Reluctantly, like so many Navajos who couldn't find work, I'd applied for welfare to pay the rent and for food stamps to feed the family. I could hear Larry Silverman's voice, an echo of disapproval in the back of my mind. "Welfare is for lazy people," he used to say. "Welfare is for bums." I picked up the check at the post office, hoping no one knew what it was. I shopped at the supermarket in Winslow, ducking my head and fumbling in my purse for the food stamps.

Anyone could fall on hard times. Anyone could need help. But on my first visit to the rez, the tribal government had promised that a good home and a good job would be waiting for me when I returned. So many months later, I still had neither one, and I talked about that with Vice President Thomas Atticity. He sighed and looked sad at the broken promise. "I'm ashamed for my people," he said, pledging to do better.

Meanwhile, I had no choice. "It's just for now," I told myself. "Just for a little while." I tried to think in the Navajo way. Among the *Dineh*, poverty was not a lack of money; it was a lack of knowledge. "He's a poor man," my aunt told me, pointing to a wealthy Navajo. "He doesn't know even one song." I was learning the songs and studying the legends. I had heard the story of how First Woman sent Heron back into the flooded underground world, telling him to dive deep into the waters and retrieve the witchcraft bundle. Unlike the *jish*, or medicine bundle, it held hurtful, not healing, objects, but they too needed to be part of the new earth world. In the old legend, the witchcraft bundle was called "the way to make money."

No one could accuse me of having such a bundle. Still, even with government help, we were barely making it. Toward the end of the month, I opened the refrigerator and found only a head of lettuce, three tomatoes, an opened tin of evaporated milk, some ketchup and mustard. On the counter was the last bit of food from the freezer—a scrawny chicken, defrosting for dinner.

I hoped it would be enough to feed two growing girls. At most meals, I heaped food on their plates, putting only token amounts on mine and Dickie's. "Why aren't you eating?" Heather sometimes asked. "Not hungry," I'd explain. Heather looked coltish and thin but, taking after Dickie, she'd always been that way. Lori, taking after me, had been chubby when we arrived, but she was now shedding some weight, standing on the bathroom scale almost every morning and gloating over every lost pound. She was freer here than she'd been in Maine, racing all over Tolani with a new flock of tribal cousins. Some days, I thought that her weight loss came from that new phyical activity; other days, I wondered if it came from poor nutrition.

Worried for my daughters, I watched closely as they explored a new territory. Now and then, they grumbled, little echos of their father's complaints, little arrows of guilt for their mother. Most of the time, as I tried to tell myself, they seemed happy enough. They too were finding a new family here, but the harmony between mind and body was elusive. Maybe we were growing in spirit, but our bodies had needs too, and I was still looking for a better way to meet them.

People told me that I could go ahead and use that census number of mine. Yet I hesitated, unsure and uncertain. The legal agency had filed my petition with the Navajo Tribal Court, asking them to recognize that I was the daughter of Betty and Yazzie Monroe, and to assign that old number to me as Yvette. But for now, that number didn't belong to Yvette. It was registered to a missing child, to a Lost Bird, to the mysterious Minnie Bob.

For Navajos, names were important, and most people had four of them. The first was a secret name whispered to a child by his or her father, and then never used, never

spoken aloud. During the years that I was missing, my father gave me such a name. As if he'd had a vision of the
life I would lead, the name was warlike. He told it to me
one day when we were alone, making me promise never to
repeat it.

As a second name, there's often a description or a nickname, sometimes serious, sometimes funny. I was *Zintkala
Nuni*, or Lost Bird. Dickie—having caught and lassoed a
dapple-gray mare, a horse he'd bought from a man who
didn't actually own it, an illegal horse he'd had to return—
was called "the white man who knows how to steal horses."
To the other children, Heather was "Puppy," because her
unruly hair tended to spike up in little dog's ears. Lori was
"Chewey," after the furry, blondish *Star Wars* creature. Sen-
sitive about her weight, seeing the nickname as a reference
to the creature's plumpness, Lori hated it. Usually, nick-
names were how you referred to people when you were
talking about them, not to them. My favorite belonged to a
raunchy, thirtyish man who was called "He Whose Genitals
Are Always Hungry."

In Navajo etiquette, there was a third name, a kinship
name, the polite one to use in face-to-face conversation. At
a first meeting, people introduced themselves by clan. "I am
Tobacco Clan," I would say, "born for Salt Clan." Then,
depending on how they were connected in the clan network,
even newly met strangers would call each other by the
proper kinship name—Mother or Father for an aunt or
uncle, Sister or Brother for a cousin, no matter how many
times removed, Daughter for a niece. Almost everyone I met
was clan-related to me. Even Albert Hale, the then-president
of the Navajo Nation, was connected to me across the generations. When we met, I stammered over the right kinship
name, finding it hard to look at this distinguished older man
and address him as "My Grandson."

The fourth name was the anglo name, the one used in

the white world, the one signed to legal documents. I was Yvette. Or maybe, after all, I was Minnie Bob.

So many things to get used to. So many changes to make. So many answers to discover. My mother, gone too soon, gone before I could find her, was a large part of those answers. I needed to know more about her. I needed to touch the reality of Betty Jackson Monroe.

"What was she like?" I asked everybody.

"Look in the mirror," said my Aunt Carrie, my mother's older sister. "You look a lot like her." My mother was dark-skinned, but some people said that she'd been taking special herbs that were supposed to lighten the skin of the child she was carrying.

Over and over, I heard the same words about my mother. She became "cold" and "mean," they said, but they understood why. She was "tough," they said, and they admired her for that. "Nothing scared her and nothing stopped her," Aunt Carrie told me. "Betty could do anything."

I began to make the movements of my mother. It was like the patterning that I'd read about for some brain-damaged children. If the child couldn't walk, people would move its arms and legs in the patterns of creeping and crawling, teaching the muscles to do the things that they'd somehow forgotten to do. They were creating new memories and sending new nerve impulses to the brain that would eventually help the child to walk. I too needed to create new synapses and make new pathways in my own brain.

So I began to move like my mother. I followed her footsteps, walking the old paths that led to the hogan where she'd lived, looking for her in the dry places that had once been meadows where she tended corn and herded sheep.

I listened to the stories that people told about her. Even among her own generation of Navajo women, who were great weavers, Betty was remembered for the rugs she wove. People say that a woman creates her own pathway of beauty as she weaves a rug. My mother did that. She was admired for the intricacy of her designs, the vividness of her colors and the amazing skill and speed that could create a six-foot rug in just a week's time. Collectors bought her rugs; interior decorators snapped them up. They sold so quickly that there were none left now in the family.

Weaving was a way to bring my mother within reach. I wanted to sit in front of a loom, moving my arms across the warp as she had, plucking at the threads with my fingers as she had. I talked about it with Katie, my older sister, the one who'd been present at my birth, the only daughter in the family who had continued the weaving tradition. "Teach me, Katie," I asked. "Please teach me." Her face opened with a wide smile. She had been waiting eagerly to teach someone, biding her time until her daughter Didi was old enough. "Of course," she said, agreeing to be my teacher. She tore a sheet of paper from a pad and made a list of the things I would need.

Long ago, I'd read about Margaret Mead as a young girl, asking her grandmother to teach her to weave. "First," the grandmother said, "you build a loom." That's where I too began. In Winslow, I found the lumber, nails, and screws that were needed to construct a traditional Navajo loom. Loran, my niece Christina's husband, volunteered to help with the building of it, and it took most of a day. Since I was my mother's daughter, we built a large frame, five feet by six feet. I was going to start small, but eventually I might make the kind of large rugs she had. The following day, Katie came to our rented house to check out the frame.

"Looks good," she told me. I was impatient to get started, but in this place everything had a story, and every homely little act had a spiritual meaning. So Katie wasn't ready yet. She wanted to sit down for coffee and a long talk. "Before you can make a rug," she explained, "you need to know what it means to follow the weaver's pathway."

My sister began to tell me the story of Spider Woman, one of the great *yei*. She reminded me that, when we visited Canyon de Chelly, I had seen the place where Spider Woman lived, the spectacular red-sandstone monolith, the landmark that soared 800 feet into the sky and was called Spider Rock. Geologists said it began to form some 230 million years ago.

All those years ago, as Katie explained, Spider Woman loved the *Dineh*. She helped the Twin Hero Gods to find Father Sun, so that he could teach them how to destroy the monsters who threatened the people in the Earth World. She taught them protection songs and gave them the magical Feather Plumes to carry as shields against danger.

After that, when the Twins had made the world safe, Spider Woman taught the people the art of weaving. She showed them how her own web could catch water and food, and how the threads could be woven close together to keep the people warm. Her own weaving loom had been made with cross poles of sky and earth cords, and with warp sticks of length-wise sun rays. When Spider Woman was weaving, it pleased Father Sky, and he would send rain as a gift.

We talked about the dreamcatcher that I'd made back in Maine, one of my first tries at figuring out what being an Indian was all about. It hung now over my bed in Tolani, a small hoop to which I'd attached a bit of silk with a webbed design, a couple of beads, and a feather. As Katie now told me, Spider Woman used to go from one baby's cradleboard to another, weaving a silken web that would attract the good dreams and keep away the nightmares. Eventually, when there were more *Dineh* babies than Spider Woman could get to, the women of the tribe began to weave their own dreamcatchers. Many people still attached the webbed design to the hoop at eight points, to represent the number of Spider Woman's legs.

Spider Woman also had another role, the Navajo version of the boogieman. "They used to warn little children that, if they didn't behave themselves, Spider Woman would come and carry them off," Katie told me. "They used to say that the top of Spider Rock was white with the bleached bones of bad little children."

Katie laughed. "I never believed that," she said. "The important thing is that Spider Woman, who is sometimes called the Wise Woman, taught us about weaving. And if you learn to be a weaver, you'll be considered a Spider Woman too."

The next day, I arrived at Katie's house, ready to begin the process of making the warp and stringing the loom. I came carrying two one-inch dowels, warp, and wrapping. Katie had two pieces of lumber to hold the dowels in place while she taught me to measure out the warp, the vertical threads. That took most of the day, a clear signal to me that weaving was going to be more of a challenge than I'd realized. Then we brought the warp back to my house and set it up on the loom. We had to connect a metal pipe to the loom, attaching one of the dowels to that and fastening the other dowel to the bottom of the frame. The warp was pulled tight, and now the weaving could begin.

Katie had a gift for me, a set of weaving tools that she'd been saving for her daughter. Maybe, when she was ready, Didi would use her mother's tools. Or maybe Katie would buy her another set. But Katie was like that, quick with a gift. I watched, wondering how I would ever repay her, as she demonstrated the next steps. She showed me how to use the dowel to lift the warp threads. Then she placed the other dowel in the warp, to keep the strings separated.

She pulled a long length from a skein of wool to start the rug. Using a heddle stick, she began. In one hand, she held the batten that would be used to beat the horizontal strands of wool, the woof, down on the warp. That same hand would lift the strings, leaving the other hand free to place the wool in the warp. I watched for a while, and then it was my turn. I was so clumsy; I couldn't seem to hold onto anything. I dropped the batten, lost hold of the wool, pulled the wrong strings. *"Klutz,"* my Jewish grandmother would have said. But Katie stayed calm and patient until, finally, I got it together. And then, lo and behold, I was actually weaving.

I had chosen basic colors, mostly earth tones, for my first rug: black and white, brown and tan, gray, red and blue. To get started, I was doing a sampler of basic designs—stripes, crystals, and diamonds. "Don't forget about leaving a break in the design," Katie told me, and I nodded. I was learning that Navajo spirituality was not a Sunday kind of thing; it was present every day, in every act. And so I needed to leave an escape route for my spirit, so that it wouldn't be trapped in the rug.

I spent hours at a time, sitting on the floor in front of my loom. I moved as my mother must have moved, my arms reaching for the wool, my fingers curling and sometimes cramping on the warp threads. I kept at it, wanting to feel what she had felt, to dream what she had dreamed. But the movements came awkwardly to me, and I made slow progress and many mistakes.

Word of my weaving spread through the rez. All of my family members stopped by, wanting to see me at work. When I went to the Trading Post, there was always a teasing question from its half-Navajo, half-Comanche owner, Stanley. "How's the rug coming along?" he wanted to know.

But something odd was happening. "You've been weaving, haven't you?" Stanley asked me one day. "Keep it up," he said. "We need the rain." Normally, in May and June, there was little or no rain in Tolani. But this year, there were often sudden drizzles and quick sprinkles of rain. By some coincidence, they seemed to come on the days when I was weaving. Maybe the legend was right. Maybe Father Sky was pleased to see the Lost Bird who was turning into a new Spider Woman. Maybe, wherever she was, my mother was looking down and was pleased too.

My first small rug took a little more than a month to finish. I was proud of having completed it, but embarrassed at what it looked like. "Next one will be better," Katie told me. Secretly, I wasn't sure about the next one. Weaving was one more step on the long road to becoming a Navajo, but the patience for it didn't come naturally to me.

Katie, though, had high hopes for the fledgling Spider Woman. Quickly, she set up a new warp so that I could start all over again. She was giving me still more glimpses into what it meant to have a big sister. "How's the weaving going?" she kept asking. When she stopped by my house, she frowned and looked displeased if she found me just sitting there, just talking with Dickie, just drinking some coffee. She shook her head. She pursed her lips and aimed them at the loom, the polite Navajo substitute for rude pointing. "Keep at it, Yvette," she kept telling me. "Keep at it."

I was still a long road away from being a Wise Woman. Katie had shown me how to weave, but I didn't learn the why of it until I drove out to the mesa to visit my Aunt Despah. She sat on the floor, perched on a cushion in front of a large loom. As she talked, her hands never stopped moving, weaving in the different colors of the woof, tamping down the threads, fingering the next row.

She barely seemed to glance at the beauty she was creating. The design was within her. "The rug is all of my experience," she told me. "It is everything that has ever happened to me, all of my history." At first, I didn't understand. "It doesn't come from the head," she explained. "It doesn't come from thinking. It comes from the hands." For the first time during that visit, she turned around to look at me. "The rug has to come from you."

I went back to work on my second rug. When I thought about what I was doing, my hands fumbled among the threads. I made mistakes, grew frustrated, and made still more mistakes. Time went slowly, and the tension knotted my back and made me wince with sharp, shooting pains.

But there were other days when I heard a voice whispering to me. "It has to come from you," the voice said. There were days when I was in the zone and I wove without thinking. I sat at the loom, unaware of time passing. My mind was open, my heart was calm, and my hands seemed to move unerringly on their own. I wove my experiences and my memories. My mother must have done that, woven thoughts of her children, and especially her stolen ones, into her own rugs. Now I put my daughters into mine, but I also moved the shuttle to the memory of my missing son, threading in the joy of Brad's birth, the delight at his first words, the hope that I always had of seeing him again one day.

The rug was large and ambitious, a design called Wide Ruins, a pattern of bright blues and greens against a gray background. I kept weaving and the rain kept coming. When I stopped at the Trading Post, Stanley grinned at me. "You're at it again," he teased. People said there was more rain that spring than they'd seen in a long time. After years of drought, there were flowers now, little blue and yellow blossoms, on the scrubby desert bushes. After one summer storm, when the thirsty soil could not absorb all the rain, the roads were flooded and impassable. Some people talked about a major weather system that was coming from the Pacific and bringing rain—El Niño. Stanley just laughed. "Uh-uh," he insisted. "It's you, Yvette."

When the rug was finished, I worried about the mistakes in it. I knew where each bad knot was. I was reluctant to show it to people but, one by one, my clan relatives arrived and insisted on seeing it. They looked at it, and they called it beautiful. Lora arrived from her home in Page. "Is it true, Yvette?" she asked. "It's only your second rug? I can't believe it." She knew of a dealer who would take the rug on consignment. I hesitated, not really wanting to part with it, mistakes and all. But the rug was made to be sold, and I needed the money that it would bring, money to buy the wool for my next rug.

Now the loom stood empty, and I tried not to look at it. The Spider Woman's hands were idle. Until the next warp was strung, something important was missing, something that linked me with my mother.

CHAPTER 10

The picture of Betty Monroe was coming clearer. I kept asking questions, and the answers seemed to tell me something about the woman I might have been.

I heard that she and Yazzie had had an arranged marriage, and family gossip had it that neither bride nor groom was enthusiastic. Betty had another suitor, another young man she would have preferred, a young man who was distraught over losing her. I listened to the story of a tragic romance. "They say that he climbed to the top of a high mesa," I was told, "and then they say that he leaped to his death."

In time, Betty and Yazzie grew to love one another. "It was a good marriage," my aunts insisted. "It was a true love." At one point, though, there were problems, and Betty put Yazzie's saddle outside the door, the Navajo gesture that signaled divorce. He returned to his own clan, but he came back, often to visit the children. During one of those visits, Betty left the door ajar, and Yazzie stepped inside, accepting her invitation to return to their marriage.

I knew now that my mother dressed in the traditional way, in a brightly colored velveteen shirt and a full mid-calf skirt, her neck and wrists adorned with silver and turquoise, her long hair swept into a neat bun. She was haunted by her missing twins, but she never stopped looking for them, and she never gave in to the harsh conditions of her life. She could bend over a wood fire and turn meager scraps into a delicious meal. She drew water from a hand pump and carried it in huge jars and cans to the two-acre garden where she grew corn and squash for her family. By hand, and later on by machine, she sewed almost all of the clothes that her family wore. She kept her home clean and her children obedient and well-mannered. She was skilled at weaving rugs and making jewelry, and she passed those arts along to her daughters.

She had all the domestic virtues that have somehow escaped me. Growing up with Bea and Larry Silverman, I was never taught to cook and clean. I was being trained to be a princess and "a lady," someone who'd always have a maid to do those things for her. Bea's portrait hung now in my Tolani living room, and Dickie still felt her eyes following him, watching him, disapproving of him. He was a good and loving man, but he knew that he was not the successful man, the moneymaker, she'd wanted for me, not the doctor, not the lawyer, not even the Indian chief.

My sisters were now trying to fill in the gaps of my education, but I was a slow learner. When we sat down for a meal at the battered kitchen table, my daughters still teased me. "Mom doesn't cook food," Heather grinned and announced one day. "She burns it."

There was more than one way, though, to follow in my mother's footsteps. The story I liked best about Betty Monroe, a story told to me by three different people, was about her fearlessness. Years ago, my birth parents raised cattle, sheep, chickens and, of course, horses. One day, Betty decided that some sheep needed to be rounded up from a distant meadow, but my father and older brothers were gone, and most of the horses with them. The only horse left was not yet tamed, still wild and spirited. There were some men working at the ranch, seasoned cowboys, but they were afraid to ride that wild horse. One by one, they refused to go after the sheep.

Betty glared at the men. Then she walked up to the horse and caught hold of its rope halter. Long skirt and all, she jumped on its bare back. The horse bucked, trying to shake her off. Betty held on. The horse kicked and reared. Betty kept her seat. She pulled sharply at the reins until, at full gallop, the horse moved out of the corral gate. Woman and beast left in a cloud of dust, and the men who stood there weren't sure when they'd see either one again. Two hours later, they were back, driving the sheep before them. Betty had a fond pat for the now-docile horse, and a tongue-lashing for the chagrined men.

This was the mother I wanted to emulate. This was the mother I'd been stolen from, the mother who never heard me laugh, and I couldn't help thinking of what might have been. If things had been different, I thought that I'd have been the child who gave her the most trouble, the one who inherited her stubbornness, the one who opposed her. But I also wanted to think that I'd have been the one most like her, the one closest to her.

I daydreamed of getting her old ranch going again. I saw myself streaking across the desert at full gallop. And then one day I saw a notice in the local newspaper. It announced that wild horses had been rounded up in the canyons and mesas. They'd been driven to Flagstaff, where anyone who wanted a horse could adopt one. "Dickie," I said, "just listen to this."

He and I weren't agreeing on much those days. He was out of medicine for his emphysema and for the arthritis that

had half-crippled his spine, and the local doctors had refused to prescribe more pills for him. They explained that
his case was too complicated for them to treat, and that he
needed a specialist. But the only specialist within a day's
drive was too busy to take on a new patient.

We talked about asking a medicine man to perform a
healing ceremony. Different medicine men were trained in
different curing ceremonies, each with its own rituals and
purpose, its own symbolism and origin legend of how the
yei gave this chantway to the people. "The only one I'd trust
is your father," Dickie insisted. But even with my father, he
shied away from the idea.

"I'm not like you, Yvette," he said. "I'm not going to
pretend to be something I'm not."

"I'm not pretending," I said, angry at the suggestion
that I was only a make-believe Navajo. "I am who I am."

"Are you sure, Yvette?" he asked. "Are you sure?"

Dickie lived each day with pain, and it made him edgy
and explosive. My heart ached for him, a good man, too
proud to complain about his bodily aches, too tormented
not to complain about *something*. He had brought me to a
place where I was finding a new peace, but it was destroying
him. Here it came, that old black feeling: Guilt. "I'm living
in hell," he told me. "I've got to get out of here." He often
felt like a man without a country, missing the familiar faces
and places of his home in Maine, feeling unwanted in a land
that didn't belong to him. "Haven't you noticed?" he asked.
"Everyone talks to you, but these people never talk to me."
It was one of those half truths. Usually, he was the one who
didn't speak, the one who wanted to be off by himself, nursing his wounded body.

"These people," he said, grumbling about Navajos,
lumping them all together. Yet he had three or four friends
who would come to the house to see him. They'd tinker
together over the engine of an aging truck. Or one of them

would lend him a horse and they'd go riding together over the dunes. On horseback, his aches and pains seemed to slip away. He loved the empty distances. He loved the people who still lived out there in the old way, without electricity, without indoor plumbing, without the mixed bag of modern influences. "The true Navajos," he called them.

His friends enjoyed Dickie and admired him. "You ride well," they told him. But they could never forget that he was a *belagaana*. "Dickie," they said, "you sure don't ride like a white man."

At home, though, when the pain had kept him up all night, Dickie was an angry man. The girls began to spend more and more nights on sleepovers at their cousins' houses. I was happy for the fun they were having and the friends they were making, but I couldn't help wishing that their own home could be more of a haven. Sometimes, the arguments turned into screaming matches. "I can't take it anymore," Dickie would begin. His moods swung wildly, and they grew worse when we got the sad news that his father, ill and fragile when we last saw him, had died.

"I can't even be there for the funeral," he said bitterly, and I understood what that meant. Years earlier, when Dickie and I were first married, Larry Silverman, my estranged adoptive father, had died of cancer before I could make it to his hospital bed to say good-bye. But I had raced to be at his funeral in Neponsit. Blanche and my stepsister pretended not to see me. They had to be told by a stranger to slip over, to make some room in the family pew for Larry's only daughter. My name was not remembered in his eulogy or in his will, but I was there, and that's what mattered. Eventually, I would receive the inheritance that counted, the box that held old family photographs and the bits and pieces of paper that turned out to be the clues to where I'd come from.

My family offered to chip in and give Dickie the money

for the airfare, but he was too hard-headed to accept it. Instead, he and I continued to argue. Sometimes he'd want to return to Maine, where his mother was now on her own and needed him. Other times, he'd want to move to someplace else warm. "Maybe Georgia," he'd say. "Maybe Florida." Or he'd want to live somewhere else on the rez. "Maybe Flagstaff, maybe Tuba City."

I loved this man, and I tried to tell myself that it was just Dickie's way. Happiness did not come naturally to him. He took it suspiciously, like a gift horse, and he always wanted to look in its mouth and find the rotten tooth. He'd always been a restless man, and I reminded myself that we'd moved half a dozen times in Maine, always hoping that the next town would be better. This time, though, I wasn't ready to start packing. My family was in Tolani, and that's where I was trying to put down new roots.

"I'm leaving," Dickie would shout. "And I'm taking the girls with me."

I knew it was the pain talking, but I couldn't stop myself from shouting back. "No you're not," I told him. "You can go if you want to, but you're not taking the girls."

When he'd wake the next morning, I'd wait to see what mood he was in. He might still want to pack up and leave. Or he might rise up smiling, his anger gone as suddenly as a spring rain. "We were right to come here," he might say. "Look how good it is for the girls." The stomach and back pains never went away, but there were days, even whole weeks, when they were bearable. And those were the times when he loved life on the rez.

"Dickie," I said, "just listen to this." When I read him the newspaper notice about the adoption of wild horses, it was one of his better days. He too wanted a horse. He too dreamed of a ranch. He too shared my almost physical need to take care of animals. We already had six baby chicks that we were raising, plus Lori's kitten and Hercules, our family dog, the furry, sweet-tempered Chow who'd come with us from Maine. We didn't have any money for more livestock, but Dickie grinned and said, "Well, it doesn't cost anything to look."

We headed for Flagstaff, our old van crowded with Dickie and me, Heather and Lori, my nieces Tina and Christina, and their five young children. Along the way, we stopped at a grain store to pick up some poultry feed and to buy four laying hens and ten meat birds to add to our flock. Poultry could be squeezed into our meager budget, especially when we told ourselves they'd save money in the long run, providing fresh eggs for breakfast and fried chicken for dinner.

In Flagstaff, we pulled into Tout Park, where the adoption of wild horses was taking place. As the children raced for the corrals, I stopped at a booth to pick up some information. The fee to adopt a wild horse was $125, a sum that left me sighing.

The horses were separated into five corrals—stallions, mares, fillies, geldings and, finally, burros. They were splendid in their wildness, nostrils flaring, eyes fiercely bright, heads proud and high. If anyone came too close to one of the horses, it would wheel, leading the other horses around it in a mini-stampede, manes flying, hooves thundering.

I moved from corral to corral, stunned by the beauty of these wild creatures. But I kept coming back to the mares. "That one," I told Dickie. "That one over there." I pointed to a black beauty, her body sleek and muscular, her forehead marked by a white arrow. I was instantly in love, and I could see that the horse had reached Dickie too.

"Oh, Dickie," I said. I was dizzy with longing. I knew that we couldn't afford it, but I also knew that he had some money with him, money for the rent and utilities we needed to pay. Yet the dream of a ranch was another strong need, and that horse could be the beginning of making the dream come true. Arm in arm, Dickie and I walked over to the booth and filled out the paperwork to adopt that horse. Then he handed over the fee, a big chunk of our rent money.

When we told Tina about it, she shook her head. "Do you have any idea what it costs to feed a horse?" she asked. But even as she raised questions, she was looking longingly at another horse, a brown mare. Dickie grinned, deciding to let tomorrow take care of itself. With her credit card, Tina got some money from an ATM, and Dickie made up the rest of her adoption fee with our utilities money.

It was irresponsible, and we knew it. It was foolish, but we couldn't help ourselves. Impulsively, we'd grabbed at a piece of our dream. Now, though, we had to find a way to move those wild horses from Flagstaff to Tolani. "How long can you hold them for us?" I asked the wrangler. He said that we needed to take delivery by noon of the next day, before the herd was shipped off to another state. We also needed a horse trailer with an enclosed roof; if these wild horses caught a glimpse of the sky, they'd see it as an escape route, and they'd jump or kick their way to freedom. Dickie, Tina, and I exchanged glances, realizing what we'd gotten ourselves into. We now had two untamed horses; they'd been in captivity for less than two months, they didn't like or trust people, and they were dangerous.

We hurried back to Tolani Lake. "Don't worry," Tina kept saying. "We can borrow a closed trailer. I know we can." We headed for the ranch, where Dickie set to work rebuilding the fences of the old corral. I joined my two nieces and all the children in picking up the nails and bits of metal that had accumulated over the years in the neglected enclosure.

It was near dusk when Tina and I remembered that we needed to find a horse trailer. We still expected that to be fairly easy. After all, almost everyone around there had horses and, with them, a trailer or two. We went to the pay phone to call the two or three people who could be reached that way, and then we drove from house to house, from hogan to hogan for the rest. At each stop, we had to explain why we needed the trailer. People looked at us, a couple of tenderfoots who'd bought some wild horses. Some people were even rude enough to laugh in our faces, instead of waiting until we turned our backs.

Of the twenty-some trailers we tracked down, all were open-roofed. I was growing nervous, and even Tina looked worried. The few closed trailers we heard about were gone with their owners to Nevada, for a big rodeo. The stars were out by the time Tina remembered still another clan member who might have a covered trailer, but definitely had no phone. We climbed into the old van and headed for the sand dunes where this person lived.

We were off on a Keystone Kops comedy of errors. "Turn here," Tina said, and we moved down a narrow dirt road. We'd gone about five miles when Tina realized we'd made the wrong turn. As we tried to turn around, though, our wheels were trapped in the sand. We backed and filled, but every move just dug us in deeper.

It was eleven on a moonless night, and we were bogged down in the middle of the desert. Tolani was twenty miles behind us, and it was ten miles to the nearest house that we knew about. The only way out was on foot, through a desert where poisonous snakes slithered in the dark, and spiders and scorpions lurked. We started hiking, with no flashlight to guide our footsteps. Then, shivering in the cold of the nighttime desert, we spotted salvation, headlights in the distance, a vehicle moving our way.

The headlights came closer, the glare blinding us. "Let's hope they're good folks," Tina whispered. A man emerged from the vehicle. "What you people doing here?" he asked gruffly. Tina and I smelled the alcohol on him and clutched hands. We didn't know how many other men were in that vehicle. Then a second man emerged, followed by a boy of about ten.

The second Navajo had no whiff of whisky about him, and I began to breathe more normally. We explained that our van was stuck in the sand. The man checked it out and told us there was no way to free that van tonight. "Could you give us a lift to Tolani?" Tina asked. The man told the boy to go back the vehicle and ask his mother what she thought about that. On big things and small, I'd noticed that Navajo men tended to consult with their women. They believed that the best answers came when you combined male and female wisdom.

While we waited for an answer, he explained that we were blocking his path to the only hogan on this little-used road. As he told us, whenever he and his wife came to spend some time at that hogan, they always got a fast-running start to carry them past the sand that had trapped us. In the headlights, we could see the boy waving us toward the vehi-cle, to meet his mother. She leaned out the passenger-side window, gesturing to us to climb into the rear. "Get in," she said, laughing. "Get in." On the way to Tolani, she asked if I knew Mrs. Bighorse. I told her that was my sister Darlena's married name. The woman smiled again. "I thought I knew you," she said. As it turned out, we'd met at the wedding of Darlena's son. Among Navajos, it was a small world, and this woman's niece had been my nephew's bride.

Arriving at my rented house, we waved good-bye to our rescuers, and they drove off to spend the night with their Tolani relatives. It was now after midnight, and I was feeling embarrassed. We'd gotten the van stuck in the desert, and I was hoping that not too many people would need to hear about that. "Please, Tina," I said, "let's keep this quiet." We decided to get a few hours sleep and then start again in the morning. My fondest wish was to get by without having to tell Dickie about our fiasco, but he awoke as I slipped into bed. Reluctantly, I began to explain but, exhausted by the long night, I fell asleep in midstory.

At five the next morning, I awoke to the sound of someone banging on the door. Still groggy, I opened it to find Tina standing there, ready to try again to dig out the van. We agreed that our best bet now was my brother Pete, with his four-wheel-drive truck. He couldn't help laughing at our woebegone story, but he was willing to help. We piled into his truck and retraced the road into the desert. With much digging, with lots of shoring up with pieces of wood, he finally managed to pull our van out of the sand.

Time was passing, though, and we still needed a horse trailer. Tina now thought of another relative who might have a covered trailer and lived just six miles away. She gave me a reassuring smile. "It's on a main road," she said. When we arrived there, two men were roping sheep. Tina spoke to them in Navajo, and they told her to speak to the owner of the truck that was parked nearby. An old woman was sitting in the driver's seat, and once again the final word would come from a woman.

The old woman tried hard to fight back the laughter, as she listened to our story. Then she called to her son, and he led us over to some corrals. There, at last, was the trailer we needed, a covered double-sized trailer that would hold our two wild horses. He hooked it to our van, and we were ready to drive off. The sound of laughter followed us, people hooting over the misadventures of two foolish women. But we were getting used to that.

Our problems seemed over. We arrived at Flagstaff just in time. We loaded the horses and headed for home. We drove through the tree-lined streets of Flagstaff and past the lush national forest at its outskirts. We were descending through the San Francisco Peaks toward the geologic bowl where Tolani lay. We passed the sign that announced that we were entering the reservation once again. This was the

barren land that the white people had allowed the Navajos
to keep. It was the place where, suddenly, the greenery
ended.

Just then, Tina and I were too happy to worry about old
grudges. We congratulated ourselves with every mile. The
laughter was now ours. "You are some cowgirl," I told Tina.
"You, too," she said, barely able to speak between giggles.

At the ranch, we backed the trailer up to the corral gate,
and unloaded the wild horses. They circled the corral,
slowly at first, then at full, powerful gallop, manes blowing
in the wind. Then they stood still, sniffing the air, eyeing
the grownups and children, the still-unfamiliar two-legged
creatures who clustered at the gate.

I don't know what they thought of us, but we thought
they were beautiful.

CHAPTER 11

I was trying to change my life by changing my stories. Forget Cinderella. Forget John Wayne. Forget Neponsit dreams of canopy beds and money in the bank. I steered the old van toward the mesa and Aunt Despah's outfit, bouncing along, watching the ruts of a washboard road. I leaned on her corral fence, my moccasins dusty with the red Tolani earth, my eyes squinting at a landscape that shimmered in the 110-degree heat of an Arizona summer. And I listened to my Aunt Despah's stories.

"The Wind won't know my name," she was saying.

She was explaining why she had never left the reservation. She was telling me what it was that kept people here on this beautiful but poor land. I was trying to plant myself in this unfamiliar territory, to feel at home on this new range. Simple survival was a challenge in this place. It fought you at every step, the earth daring you to try to grow something. But for Navajos, this Earth was our mother, this Sky was our father. And this Wind, blowing in from the mesa, was a Holy Spirit.

The Holy Wind, as Aunt Despah told me, gives life, thought, and speech to the people who live between the four sacred mountains. If you lived beyond those borders, the Wind would not know who you were and could not help you. The Holy Wind Spirit could not send a small wind to sit at your ears—like the angel that some white people think sits on their shoulders—and whisper advice on what to do.

My questions were practical. Generation after generation, my family had lived the hard life of the reservation. All six of my sisters and brothers had stayed on, or very close to, the rez. Outside its borders, there were strangers who looked down on Navajos and disrespected their ways. But there were also more comforts, better jobs, and greater opportunities. There was the chance of an easier life. "Easier, yes," my aunt said, "but maybe not better."

I was trying to understand what had drawn me to this place. To do that, I needed to know what made my family stick it out on the rez. In the Navajo way, my Aunt Despah had spiritual answers. "We have to be in this place," she told me. She explained that the *Dineh* were related to the four-legged creatures and the winged ones, to Father Sky and Mother Earth, and to all the Holy People. "They are all our relatives. We know them, and they know us. And so how can we move?" she asked. "How can we leave our relatives behind?"

She scanned the landscape, the only scenery she has ever known, full of the holy places that define a Navajo, the red rocks, the blue canyons, the formations formed by wind and time into the Navajos' cathedrals. And then she smiled at me. "We don't understand about packing up and moving away," she explained. "We have no Navajo word for relocating. For us, if you go beyond the four mountains, it's as if you had disappeared. It's what happened to you, Minnie Bob," she explained, calling me by my birth name. "They took you away. You disappeared. All those years, you felt lost and incomplete, and it was because the Wind did not know your name."

Was that it? Answers blowing in the wind? So far, I heard only silence. Maybe it took practice to catch the whispers of that small wind at one's ears. Growing up as Larry Silverman's daughter, I'd been taught to be a tinkerer, forever taking things apart to see how they worked. Wherever I lived, in New York, in Israel, in Maine, I believed in what I could touch with my own hands and see with my own eyes. But now I'd come to live with people who looked at the world with different eyes, and they found their explanations in things you could sense but not always see and hardly ever touch.

A part of me was still missing. Maybe it took wholeness to hear the Wind. Wherever he was, if Aunt Despah was right, the Wind still did not know my lost brother's name. And neither did I.

A few days later, my sister Lora and I sat at the kitchen table, scraps of paper spread out before us, communiques from that second man who thought he might be my twin brother. "No way," Lora was saying in that soft voice of hers. "No way. It's not him." We shuffled the papers, reading them over and over. We hoped for facts that would fit. We longed for dates and places that would match. "It's not him," Lora repeated. "But he keeps writing. He keeps calling." Half a year ago, half a lifetime ago, I'd been afraid to say yes to my new identity. Now this man didn't want to take no for his own answer.

For Lora, the clincher was the man's photograph. "He doesn't look like anyone in our family," she said. And that wasn't all. The man had posed in a short-sleeved shirt, unbuttoned to show the dark curly hairs of his chest. "Just look at all that hair," Lora said, shaking her head. "On his arms. On his chest." If my own once-blond hair had raised questions, this man's abundant dark hair was an even bigger problem. "It can't be our brother," Lora said. She was laughing. "No way. No Navajo has so much hair on his body." She gathered up the papers. "We have a lot of different names for the *belagaana*," she said, still laughing. "And one of them is Hairy Man."

Two candidates down. How many more to go? I fought against the discouragement. In this dry stretch of the reservation, anything that grows does so by contrariness. It takes patience and faith to survive here, and I was trying to train my brain in those paths. My family had persisted in their search for me, and that stubbornness was in my genes. I would not stop looking for my brother. My message was still posted on the Internet. Along with modern technology, though, I turned to my father. And I asked him to search in the Navajo way.

We gathered in the hogan, a family circle of sisters and brothers, nieces, nephews, and cousins. We sat cross-legged on the floor, not touching, not holding hands, connected by something stronger than the physical, the old rhythms that my father was chanting. *Neya heya heya'ya.* I could only hope that the Wind was listening. Finally, at nightfall, my father led us out of the hogan and, in a caravan of vans and pickup trucks, we drove out into the desert.

The sky stretched forever, a velvety blue-black canopy, hung with stars and the silver crescent of a waning moon. The men built a campfire and we gathered around it, seated once again in a unifying circle. My father began to chant more prayers. He blessed each of us. He took a dark cloth from his *jish* and spread it on the ground in front of him. Then he placed a large crystal on that cloth. In silence, he stared into the crystal.

I tried, as I'd been told, to clear my mind. I tried to concentrate. For a quick second, I was a child again, sitting in the dark around a Ouija board. Then I felt how different, how solemn this desert moment was. Years ago, when I was lost in a white world, my family had searched for me with this same ceremony. Now, here I was, a part of the circle, one of the searchers. We were trying to make a connection to my brother, trying to see him.

No one spoke. If my brother was alive, we might be able to reach his spirit. No one stirred. If it was night wherever my brother was, if he was asleep, he might hear us calling in his dreams. My whole being was centered on that. I don't know how much time passed. Then, in the stillness of the desert, I saw a vivid picture, not in the crystal but in my mind.

I saw a man the same age as me, a dark-skinned man, strangely familiar, standing by a river. I could see the thick roots of a great tree that grew by that river. The man was looking toward the woods, as if he were waiting for someone. Then he turned away. I saw him kneel down, cup his hands, and drink from the river.

I didn't believe in such things. I had always told myself that the moment in the movie theater, the instant when Bea spoke to me, was an anomaly, a once-in-a-lifetime event, something that happened because we were so close. But my brother was a stranger, appearing now in my mind's eye. As the scene unfolded, I looked up at the night sky. A bright star shone just under the moon. Then I saw another star, a dimmer one, moving across the sky to join the bright one, and then moving away. The dimmer star moved across the sky three times, and then it disappeared.

Stars do not move back and forth in the sky. People cannot be seen across time and space. I knew that, but I also knew what I had just seen. My father stood and broke the spell. He returned the crystal to his *jish*. "I saw a man waiting by a river," I said. Before I could mention the trees, my father spoke. "There was a great tree," he said, "with big roots coming out of the ground." Someone else talked of how the dark man had knelt down to touch the water. All of us had seen the same man, the same tree, the same star moving across the night sky. All of us, even skeptical Dickie, saw those same things.

Seeing was believing. Or, as the Navajos said, believing was seeing. "My son will return to us," my father said. He looked at me. "Maybe two years, maybe three, and then your brother will come home."

I drove home in a jumble of thoughts and emotions, steering the old van along the jouncing reality of a rutted road. I was enough of a Navajo to believe that I had seen my brother during that ceremony, and to feel awed and elated by that. But I was still morphing, a part of me still an impatient New Yorker. My father had said "two or three years," a long time to wait. I was not yet Navajo enough to just say, "Okay. So be it."

It was close to dawn when we returned home from that ceremony. A few hours later, there was more news of my brother. Calvin Nez arrived at my door. He was a wiry old man, walking with a cane and wearing a broad-brimmed, black-felt hat. He was the father-in-law of my brother Pete, and he lived far out, past the mesa, with no electricity or running water. I'd met him for the first time the previous day, when I'd helped Pete to haul two 100-gallon tanks of water to Calvin's old hogan. We'd said ya'at eh and shaken hands. Later on, Pete told me that Calvin was a Hand Trembler, the kind of medicine man who used touch to diagnose an illness and, at times, to see into the future.

"You saw your brother last night, didn't you?" Calvin asked. No one had told him that my father was going to perform a ceremony. No one had talked to him about the outcome of that ceremony. All that had happened was the quick touch of my hand the day before. Yet somehow he knew. "You saw the stars, didn't you?" he asked. As Calvin understood it, the bright star represented me, and the dimmer one was my brother, still missing, still lost. We had crossed paths three times in our lives, according to Calvin, and we were destined to come together again. "Your brother will find his way back," the Hand Trembler said. "But it won't be two or three years. It won't be that long. It could be one year. It could be 1998."

I smiled, not sure what to believe. Listening to the stories and prophecies, I was not ready to swallow them whole, not quite, not yet. But I was taking them in. Like the daily fry bread and the constant mutton stew, they were becoming a part of me.

"It's going to be a good day," I told Dickie, offering my own prophecy. It was still early morning, and I'd been up all night at the ceremony. But I was smiling, even humming as I washed the breakfast dishes, and awaited the arrival of my landlady. Mary spoke no English and I had only a dozen words of Navajo, but she turned up every morning, sat down at my table and drank a cup of coffee. She beamed at me. I smiled back. And that was our conversation. "She's in our clan," Katie explained one day. "So she's your clan mother, and she wants to get to know you."

That day, though, was different. Mary was beaming more broadly than ever, and she had no time for coffee. "Lori," she said. "Lori," she repeated. School was out that day, and Lori was curled up in blankets on the living room couch, still half-asleep. She was slimmer now, losing her baby-fat, and the sun had turned her hair blonder than ever.

For my daughters, Mary was a clan grandmother or *shi ma sonn*, and that's what that day's visit was about. Lori stretched, yawned and, when she saw Mary, came wide awake. Quickly, she was in her clothes. Then Mary gave her a hug and pushed her out the front door.

I was puzzled, with no idea what Mary wanted my daughter for. But Lori and Mary had a special relationship, one that made me smile even as it baffled me. One of them jabbered away in English, the other in Navajo. Somehow, across the languages and across the generations, they understood one another. A half hour later, Lori was back with an answer to the mystery, and with a grin that split her face like a sunrise. "Guess what?" she said. "Grandma Mary gave me a present. You won't believe what it is. It's two goats!"

For a Navajo, it was an amazing present and a great honor. Taking care of one's herd was part of the Navajo way of being in this world, and Navajos did not like to sell or give away their animals. Livestock were the measure of wealth, the source of food and of wool for clothing, blankets, and rugs. As Dickie and I had been told, if we ever had the money to buy some livestock, no Navajo would want to sell us their goats or sheep. We'd have to go shopping among white people or Mexicans.

Yet Mary had given Lori a gift of two goats, a male and a female. She'd made Lori promise to keep them for at least four years, so that they could produce the offspring that would be the beginning of Lori's herd. "That way, you will have food always," Mary told her, "and wool from the goats."

We loaded the goats into our van and drove to the ranch. There, we herded them into an old pen, the same pen where my mother had once kept her own goats and sheep. But Lori was just getting started. A couple of months earlier, my Aunt Despah had promised to give her a sheep one day. "Okay," Lori announced. "Now let's go get Aunt Despah's sheep."

This too was a great gift. Many years ago, a Navajo's identity—and his survival—depended on large herds of sheep, but in the 1930's, claiming that the land could no longer support so many animals, the federal government ordered a stock reduction. Navajos watched, weeping at the waste and sacrilege, as federal agents shot or starved the "excess animals." The grandmothers and grandfathers still told the young children about that, and the pain was still fresh. These days, you needed a permit to graze a limited number of sheep, and those grazing permits were often the most valuable thing that a Navajo might have to leave to his or her children.

"Let's go, Mom," Lori kept saying. I shook my head at her. I tried to explain that it would be rude to ask for the sheep before my aunt was ready to give it, but Lori was having none of that. "Let's go, Mom," she kept nagging. She was too impatient to stand on polite ceremony. "Let's go," she insisted, tugging at my arms.

"*Beseder*," I said, lapsing into Hebrew. "Enough." I still spoke more Hebrew than Navajo. The new language baffled me with its glottal stops. The old language was usually a sign to my daughters that I was serious about what I was saying. *Beseder* usually meant "I've had it, girls." But stubborn Lori wasn't reading signs that day, and she kept at me until I gave in.

We drove to Aunt Despah's house. She was sitting on the floor in front of her loom, weaving a six-by-eight foot rug. Her husband John was sitting on the couch, watching TV, and her daughter-in-law was bent over a table, creating sand paintings for sale to tourists. *Ya'at eh*'s all around. Handshakes all around. Then, sending Lori outside to play, I sat down next to my aunt.

I was planning to do this the Navajo way, have a visit, talk for a while and then, just as I was about to leave, ask for the sheep. We talked about Despah's rug. I asked about her health and her family's health. I wondered how life was treating her. I was still a long way from mentioning the sheep when Lori burst back in. "Well," she demanded, "did you ask her yet?"

"Ask me what?" Despah wondered. Feeling embarrassed, I began to explain. I hoped that my aunt wouldn't think I was raising Lori without manners. Despah listened and began to laugh. "It's okay," she said. "It's okay. But the sheep are out in the field. About a quarter mile away. Lori, you'll have to round them up first."

Until that moment, my daughter had never herded anything in her life. Despah, John, and I went outside to watch the event. "You have to get behind the sheep . . ." Despah began to explain. But Lori, impatient for her sheep, wasn't listening. She took off, racing toward the grazing sheep. "Get behind them," I shouted, but Lori had run right into the center of the herd. One moment the sheep were nibbling quietly at the patches of scrub grass. The next moment, startled by Lori, they were stampeding at full speed in the wrong direction.

Lori's face was a map of surprise and frustration. Then, more determined than ever, she raced to catch up with them. "Get behind them," I kept shouting. Finally she understood. She moved to the rear of the sheep. In position at last, she shooed the sheep together. "Whooshie, whooshie," she kept yelling. Zig-zagging behind the strays, she managed to herd them toward the pen.

Lori and I were breathless, she from running after the sheep, me from laughing. Despah culled the promised gift, a young female sheep, from the herd. We loaded her into the van and drove back to the ranch. Then we put the ewe in the pen with the goats. The Melanson family now had one horse, two goats, one sheep, assorted poultry, one dog, and two cats. Our animal count had soared in just one day, and the dream of a reborn ranch was just a bit closer, and looking just a bit more possible.

The Black One, as we called the horse, was still untamed. I'd ridden horses back when I was Bea Silverman's little princess, going to sleepaway camp every summer, but it was Dickie who was truly savvy about horses. He'd managed to calm the Black One down to the point where she'd eat a carrot from his hand. Sometimes, she'd stand still while the girls leaned across the corral fence to pet her. She'd allow herself to be led around the corral by a lead rope, but only if you managed to slip on the rope without her seeing it. If she caught sight of the rope, it spooked her. Her eyes rolled wildly in her head, and she lashed out with her hooves.

We asked a clan relative to finish the Black One's training and get her ready to be ridden. He was a lean, sun-darkened man with the bowlegs of a longtime cowboy, standing at the corral gate, studying the horse for a long moment. Then he approached, rope in hand. The Black One caught sight of it. She pawed at the earth. She reared up, kicking out with her front legs. Her neighs were like trumpet blasts. Her eyes were wild and fearsome as she bucked, lashing out with her hind legs.

She began to circle the corral, picking up speed with each long stride. The corral fence stood six and a half feet high but, in one great leap, she cleared it. She was free, racing for the desert. The trainer jumped on his horse, galloping after her. Riding my niece Tina's horse, Dickie joined the chase. But the Black One was too fast. She was a dark streak racing across the flatland and disappearing into the horizon.

That night, there was mourning in the Melanson house. But the next morning, Dickie and I went in search of our missing mustang. Family members and friends, even a few strangers, joined in to help us. We were an odd, makeshift posse, some of us on horseback, some in vans, a few on motorcycles. We followed the narrow roads that snaked through the desert. When there were no roads, we made our own paths in the sand. We searched day after day, going further and further into the desert. "The next dune," I kept thinking. "Maybe she's behind the next dune." Each day, the wind flattened old dunes and whipped new dunes into shape. But the Black One was nowhere to be found.

On the sixth day, there was a last-gasp search party—Dickie, a clan relative, a nine-year-old nephew, and my Lori, riding a borrowed pony. Followed by a trailer with two spare horses, they headed for the sand dunes. They'd been searching for almost four hours when, at last, there she was. The Black One was standing still, but poised to break away at any moment. She was still wild, still skittish, still too wary of a rope for anyone to think about trying to lasso her. Dickie approached slowly, grabbing a handful of sand grass as a peace offering. With one hand, he tempted her with the grass. With the other hand, he managed to catch on to the remnants of her lead rope. Her halter was halfway off her dark head, one ear completely out of it.

Slowly, talking quietly to her at each step, Dickie led the Black One out of the sand dunes. They'd covered about three miles when they came to a house with a corral and a loading chute. Dickie led the Black One into the loading chute, calming her as he fixed the halter. He removed the old and shredded lead rope and attached a fresh one to the halter. Then he tied her to the back of the trailer and, driving slowly, the search party covered the seven miles to our ranch.

For a few days, searching for the Black One, Dickie seemed to forget his aches and pains. He found a new strength and a new pride. My family had been teasing him, making jokes about a *belagaana* who thought he was going to tame a wild horse. But he was the one who'd had the sharp eyes to find the Black One and the gentle hands to bring her home. "Watch it, Dickie," one of his friends teased. "People could start thinking that you're part Navajo."

Running away seemed to have changed the Black One too. She'd left some of her wildness out on the desert. Before long, she'd be ready to be ridden. Dickie and I had decided that she was not to be broken; she was to be gentled. Every day, we drove to the corral at the ranch, bringing hay, soft touches, and encouraging words. We were catching on to another Navajo idea. In the white world, nature was a chal-

lenge, something to be overcome and conquered. For Navajos, nature was a responsibility, something to be taken care
of, something to live in harmony with.

Some days, the Black One still backed off nervously.
Other days, she allowed herself to be led around the corral,
head high, eyes liquid-brown and calm. I stroked her soft
nose and whispered into her ear. "The day is coming," I
told her. Before much longer, I would heave a saddle onto
her back and cinch it tight. Or maybe I would do without
the saddle. Maybe I would gallop across the desert, riding
bareback. Long hair flying in the wind, I would be Betty
Monroe's long-lost daughter, home at last.

CHAPTER 12

Omens. I wasn't sure about believing in them, but I was collecting them. Like the charms on a bracelet. Or like the feathers and crystals of a medicine bundle.

Window Rock was falling down. Chunks of rock and shale had come thundering to the ground at midday, torn from the sacred stone formation that marked the capital of the Navajo Nation. The great circle, the natural window carved by the centuries, was still intact. It still towered to the east, framing the early morning sun. But the *Dineh* saw the landslide as a warning. Geologists shrugged and said that these things happen from time to time, but the people were uneasy.

Formations like Window Rock are shaped by the winds, the rains, and the passing centuries, and they have a religious significance, representing the interior of the earth, the place from which the First Beings emerged. Window Rock also stood for something else. In 1864, it was where Kit Carson and his cavalry rounded up thousands of Navajos, ending the Southwest wars between red and white, leading the defeated people on the "Long Walk" toward the cruel imprisonment at Bosque Redondo and the terrible years that Navajos still talked about as if they were only yesterday. The return to Window Rock, like the Jewish return to Jerusalem from captivity in Babylon, symbolized the end of that lonely exile.

Medicine people gathered at the foot of Window Rock to diagnose the cause of the landslide and ponder its meaning. "The people are divided," they concluded. "The people are arguing." The medicine people were talking about politics. Within the tribal government, there were heated arguments over how to bring jobs to the reservation in a way that didn't threaten tradition and didn't gouge great scars into Mother Earth.

I took the omen personally. On good days, Dickie would still remember how to laugh. He would scoop up the girls for a drive to the ranch, teasing all the way, spending time with the animals he and they loved. Some nights, when the girls were in bed, he would take my hand and lead me out for a walk under the desert stars. But on some bad days, life among the Melansons looked like the rubble at the bottom of Window Rock.

More and more, my family was arguing. "Put a beanie on your head, Yvette, and you're Jewish," Dickie taunted. "Put a feather in your hair and you're an Indian." My family was divided. The girls listened to our quarrels, and they began to play mom against dad. They were growing slow to listen and quick to talk back.

Dickie talked partly out of pain, partly out of lifelong habit. He put things bluntly. "There are two camps in this family," he told me. "There's you and Heather, both of you liking the life here, and then there's me and Lori."

Lori was the daughter who looked like me and grumbled like Dickie. Making a face, she pulled angrily at her blond hair. "Maybe," she suggested, over and over, "I should dye it black." And there it was again, the familiar twinge of guilt, the self-blame for bringing an eleven-year-old to a place where it would be so hard to be different.

"I don't like it here," she complained, sulking on the couch. "I have no friends here," she said, forgetting about all the children who came knocking at our door, eager for her company, wanting to play with her. She was finding it hard to adjust her eyes to the Tolani landscape, and she longed for trees and greenery. She dreamed of water, and so did Heather. "When I grow up," Heather had already told me, "I'm going to California to be a marine biologist." Lori had her own plans. "I'm moving to Florida," she always said, "to swim with the dolphins and the sharks."

Lori sat there, burrowing into the pillows of the couch, making a sad face as she stroked her cat. An animal-lover, a devoted shepardess to her mini-flock of goats and sheep, she worried about the way some of our neighbors let their dogs and cats run free and wild and, without money for bags of Alpo, find food for themelves. "They're mean to animals here," she announced.

Nature was sometimes raw and cruel, and our little flock of chickens had fallen prey to those hungry, roaming dogs. Dickie saw it happen. "All of a sudden, those dogs were there," he told me afterward. "They were pouncing on the chickens. I ran outside. I didn't even have time to put my pants on. I ran outside in my underwear, looking like a fool. If any of your Navajos saw me, they must have thought I was some crazy white man, out there in his underwear." Dickie, a modest man, was half embarrassed, half angry. "There was a whole pack of those dogs, and by the time I chased them away, it was too late to save the chickens."

I cleaned up the ugly scene. Lori was weeping over the lost chicks, and I too felt like crying. Sometimes nature itself seemed out of harmony. "It's not nature," Dickie insisted.

"It's those people, those Navajos. They're just too mean or too lazy to look after their own animals." But Dickie was a complicated man. The dogs had gotten one of our turkeys too, and Dickie was picking carefully among the scattered feathers. He was grumbling about "those Navajos," but he was saving the best feathers for them, the ones they might want to hang on a dreamcatcher or use in a ceremony.

Fitting in was tricky, and some white-world ideas were hard to give up. Our dog Hercules and our two cats were indoor animals, pampered house pets, and some of our relatives and neighbors scratched their heads over that. "What's that dog doing inside the house?" they wanted to know. "What's that cat doing on the couch?" By tradition, most Navajos kept their dogs and cats outside the house, where their job was to watch for the approach of evil spirits and warn the family. I tried to explain that, but to Lori and Dickie, it was just one more thing that was wrong with the rez.

"These people," Dickie muttered. "These Navajos." I listened and I sighed. There was a good man behind that bad mouth, but there were days when I thought about his saddle, his most prized possession, on display in the bedroom, constantly oiled and buffed to show off its tooled leather. There were days when I thought seriously about putting that saddle out the door.

Driving to the ranch to feed the horses, bouncing along the rutted road, Dickie and I talked about our differences. A stiff wind was blowing across the desert, whipping up spirals of sand, chasing those spirals across the flat landscape. The Navajos called them "dust devils," and one of them was whirling in my path, just ahead of me. "It's nothing," I thought, planning to drive right through it. "Just some sand, just some air." But I was not prepared for the force of the wind in that dust-devil. When the van collided

with it, there was a great, shuddering thump. The van
rocked and veered, and I had to struggle to stay on the road.

Dickie and I shared an amazed look. Then we went back
to talking about our problems. We had home-brewed wind-
storms to get through, and I did not want to be knocked off
my Navajo road. I was weary of arguing, and maybe he was
too. "Truce?" I offered, longing for an end to turbulence.
Dickie's mood always brightened as he neared the animals
he loved. "Sure," he grinned. "Where's the peace pipe? Got
one on you?"

We needed to put our heads together. Somehow, we
needed to find a way to make the rez work for my pouting
daughter and my restless, unhappy husband. "I worry about
you, Yvette," Dickie was saying, "and I worry about the
girls." I nodded. "I know," I whispered. Part of what I
would always love about him was the way he had of making me feel safe and protected. "I'm the kind of man who
says what he thinks," he went on. Then he gave me a quick,
wry smile. "But you know, Yvette, that I don't mean half of
what I say." He's rock-ribbed conservative, shy about being
kissed in the daylight, even by his wife, even out in the
desert where there was no one to see, but I leaned over
and did just that. I was feeling better now, feeling surer of
the future.

There was another omen, one that I also took personally.
A white buffalo had appeared in the west. It was a rare
event and, for Native Americans of many different tribes, it
was the fulfillment of an ancient prophecy that foretold the
return of peace and harmony. Tens of thousands of people
had traveled to the Wisconsin farm where the buffalo calf
was born. They left feathers, necklaces, and other offerings.
One man left the medal that he'd won in Vietnam. Even
rarer than the birth of a white buffalo was the news that
this one was not just a genetic abnormality, not just an al-
bino. This one had changed colors four times, from white to

tan to brown to black, something that the elders said happened only once or twice in a hundred years.

The buffalo was female and, just as in the prophecy, the bull that sired her had died. They gave her a name—Miracle. Her four colors signified the four directions and the four poles of the traditional hogan. They represented the four sacred mountains of the *Dinetah* and the four peoples of the earth—red, white, yellow, and black. For Native Americans, it was an omen of new unity. People told me that it was also a sign that the missing children would soon be coming home.

"My lost brother," I thought. For me, it was one more revelation to add to the visions of my father and the prophecy of the Hand Trembler.

But then there was a third omen, a less happy one, my past in collision with my future.

At long last, in September, moving day arrived. We gathered up the bits and pieces of old furniture that we'd hauled all the way from Maine. We packed them into the back of the van and the bed of a borrowed pickup truck. The last thing to go in was Bea's portrait, wrapped carefully in a blanket.

Without a backward glance, we drove the short distance from the little rental house to a new one in the grid of houses from which the ghosts had been chased. We opened the door onto newly sanded floors and walls that were thin but sparkling with fresh white paint. There was a fully equipped kitchen, two baths, and four bedrooms—one for Dickie and me, one apiece for the girls, and even one to spare. "Thank you, God. Thank you." The front windows looked out onto paved sidewalks that led to the homes of half a dozen of my closest relatives. The rear windows offered a clear view of the desert, stretching toward the mesa, looking golden that day under a cloudless blue sky.

"This is it," I thought. "This is the beginning of real life in this place."

Our front door faced in the traditional direction—east. Just across the road, my niece Gail had also moved into one of the new houses, but her front door opened in the wrong direction. Instead, she had to shoo her children out the back door each morning, to catch their dawn blessing. Each morning, at another nearby house, a man could be seen climbing out of a window. "Hmm, some hanky-panky going on," we thought at first. But he was not a midnight lover, just a Navajo with no door, front or back, that faced east. The builders had been told how important an eastern exit was. Maybe they thought it was just superstition. Maybe this was just another example of white insensitivity to native traditions.

Bea's portrait, still wrapped in a blanket, went into the back of a closet in Heather's new room. "Until I can figure out where to hang it," I said. But a week or so later, when I pulled it out of the closet and unwrapped it, Bea's portrait was broken. The glass that had protected her beautiful face for all those years was shattered.

Was this an omen too? My hands shook as I picked away the shards of glass. I had carried this portrait, my most cherished possession, with me to so many different places. I had kept it safe for so many years. Carefully, I wrapped the splinters of glass in newspapers and carried them to the waste bin. I stared at the portrait, looking into Bea's eyes and feeling a great sadness, like someone saying a long good-bye.

Was this a message? The broken glass could be replaced, when there was money, when there was time, when I had finished arranging the furniture of my new life. My Navajo family understood the love that I would always feel for Bea. But they also worried that there were people, living or dead, wanting to pull me back to the white world. Maybe they were right. Maybe the past needed to be put away, stored in the back of a closet, at least until I had sorted out the present.

We were living now under different eyes, loving but also watchful. A steady parade of sisters and aunts, nieces and little cousins, strolled down the sidewalks and came through my front door. The grownups wanted coffee and a chat. The children wanted Heather and Lori for games of Shadow Tag and Spotlight Murder, a Navajo version of hide-and-seek, played with flashlights.

My sister Katie took to stopping by on her way to her job as a teacher at Tolani's hogan-shaped preschool. Dickie, the resident insomniac, would have been awake for hours by the time she arrived. He'd have the coffee pot going, and he would pour a cup for her. "Where's Yvette?" she always asked. I was the resident night owl, late to bed and still dozing at half-past seven.

Through the thin walls, I could hear the murmur of their voices. One morning, Katie left Dickie in the living room and followed the hallway that led to my bedroom. "Yvette?" she called out, knocking at the door. "Why are you still in bed?" She was my big sister, filling in for a mother who was gone. In Navajo tradition, she had the right, even the duty, to instruct me in the correct ways to lead my life.

"The day's half gone," she announced. I had missed the dawn, missed the sunrise prayers, missed the blessing of the Holy People as they passed by. I'd left a book open on the couch and my shoes in front of it. There were some clothes, mine and the girls', scattered here and there. Katie frowned and fretted over that. The Holy People might think that I had too many possessions, more things than could fit in my closets, and they might take that as a sign that I didn't need a blessing after all.

I was a casual housekeeper, but Navajos are serious about neatness and sticklers over cleanliness. In the afternoon, my cousin Irene arrived, a sweet, plump woman. She said *"Ya'at eh,"* and then sat down on my old flowered couch. Her television set was broken and, without a dish, only a lone channel came in on mine. Luckily, it was the one that showed her favorite soap opera. "I need to know what's happening to those people," she explained. During a commercial, her eyes wandered. The desert sand was a constant, drifting in through the door, seeping in through the windows. "Yvette," she told me, "you really need to clean your floors."

An army of relatives was telling me what to do. If they were older than me, it was their right. They munched on my fry bread and offered advice. "Next time," they said, "more salt." If they were younger, they were more subtle. "Yvette," a niece said, smiling at me, "those ants have made a really good home in that corner."

I was surprised at my own feelings about that. In my previous life, I'd have bristled at being bossed around. In my new life, I accepted it. Somehow, I wasn't annoyed or offended. Somehow, I took it as a sign of caring and concern. I was a Navajo-in-training, a slow learner, and they were my teachers, marking the papers of my life with lots of red pencillings.

In turn, they accepted me, even when I did the unacceptable. I looked people in the eye, a social error. I spoke without thinking, a major sin. I argued with my elders, a Navajo taboo. "You're wrong," I told Aunt Despah one day. "Just plain wrong." Katie was there, and I caught the look of shock on her face. But Despah let it pass. "If I did that, she wouldn't talk to me for a year," Katie told me later. "But she sees that you don't know any better."

I was rez'ed out, as they called it, dressed in faded jeans and an oversize tee-shirt, looking like everybody else. But wherever I went, I stood out as a newcomer. "Navajos are quiet people. If we don't understand something, we just sit there in silence. We don't ask questions," my sister Lora explained. "But you, you're always asking questions." She smiled at me. "It's okay for now," she said. "We understand that you need some answers."

I did need answers, and some important ones came when I attended my first Squaw Dance.

"Squaw" is an impolite word, a rude way to refer to a woman, though Navajos sometimes use it themselves. A Squaw Dance is an Enemy Way or *'Anaa'ji*, a ceremony that was first used to protect warriors from the ghosts of the enemies they'd killed in battle. Over the long decades, it grew into a four-day ceremony for anyone who was haunted by the ghosts of white people, or Hopis and other non-Navajos, or by the specters of witches, violence, or other hideous traumas.

Like any Navajo happening, a Squaw Dance was a mix of the spiritual and the material, the ethereal and the mundane. Two clans had joined together for this one, my Tobacco Clan and another, each connected by blood or marriage to the "patient" in need of healing, each with a camp of its own at some distance from the other. Almost four hundred people, every relative who could make it, would attend the ceremony, and it would take dozens of sheep to feed them all.

I parked my van among the multitude of other vans, trucks, and cars. Someone handed me a knife and gave me a little push toward the waiting sheep. It was a bloody, primeval scene, with women and men alike doing the slaughtering. My job was to help carve the sides of sheep into sections for roasts, stews, and soups. Other women were already bent over cooking fires, and the men were busy building brush arbors and other shelters for the guests. We worked all through the day, sweating over the stews, shaping the fry bread, joking and gossiping.

By twilight, the food was ready and there was something electric in the air, a sense of anticipation that I didn't understand. "Over there," my sister Katie was saying. "The other clan is coming." In the distance, I could see a great cloud of dust moving toward us. We waited, hushed and expectant. Then I could hear the sound of hoofbeats, like rolling thunder, coming closer and closer for the Encounter of the Camps, as it was called.

Out of the dust came horses, more than fifty of them, their riders urging them on faster and faster. They were coming at us at full gallop, an astonishing, heart-stopping spectacle. Then, at the last possible moment, they swerved, still at great speed, and circled our camp four times. Finally they stopped, hard-breathing horses and proud riders framed against a sky that was turning red and purple in the sunset.

Behind the horses came a great fleet of trucks, vans, and cars, stopping close to us. No one dismounted. No one left their vehicles. "Get ready," Katie told me. The dust had cleared, and I realized that skeins of yarn were attached to saddles and bridles, door handles and truck antennae. It was another Navajo gift-giving. Some of the women began to sing, a signal for all of the women to run among the horses and the vehicles, snatching up as much yarn as each could carry.

With their gifts accepted, the riders dismounted. They greeted old friends. They moved among the cooking fires, and the feasting began. Hundreds of people were there to give their support to a ceremony they could not see, a mystery that was taking place out of our sight.

All this time, the "patient" had been sequestered in the ceremonial hogan, the *hataali* with him, preparing for the chantway that would begin at sunset and last until dawn. Within the hogan, the *hataali* was creating a great sand painting, using colored sands and crushed minerals to depict the symbols and holy figures that were connected to the hoped-for healing. Only the patient, his wife, and his eldest son—representing First Man, First Woman, and First Child—were allowed to be present inside the hogan, and the sacred details of the ceremony were an ancient, closely guarded secret.

During the night, the *hataali* would use corn pollen and sage, prayer sticks and eagle feathers, cedar smoke and wild mountain tobacco. He would sing, not prayers of supplication or pleas for healing, but songs of the emergence and stories of the creation, ancient words meant to restore a person's harmony with his mind and body, his community and his land.

Outside the hogan, women stood in clusters, gossiping and catching up on one another's lives. Men lounged against their pickups, smoking and drinking colas. A circle formed, and the dancing began. The tradition of the Squaw Dance started with young men returning from battle. Over the decades, it evolved into the Navajo version of an Anglo coming-out party, with parents bringing their marriageable daughters to meet those young men. In their best velveteen dresses and finest turquoise necklaces, the young women were signaling that they were ready and willing to be courted and to become someone's bride.

At a Squaw Dance, it was ladies' choice. As the drumbeats began, loud and insistent, the women moved to choose their partners. A woman could tug at any man's arm, and he had to accept her invitation to dance. There was no refusing, and there was only one taboo. A woman could not choose a man who belonged to the same clan as she did. A simple dance with even a distant relative was considered to be a flirtation with incest.

Different clans have different Squaw Dance traditions. In our clan, the tradition was that the man thanked the

woman for the dance by giving her a token payment, usually
one dollar. My daughters were flushed with excitement.
Even young girls like Heather and Lori, still not of marriageable age, could pick out a partner and tug at his arm. "Look
at this, Mom," Heather said, eyes shining. After a few
dances, after checking with an aunt to see which men were
unrelated and thus kosher, she had a fistful of dollars.

Like most things Navajo, it was a mix of the secular and
the sacred. I stood on the sidelines, watching the dancers
move in the circle. Dickie had stayed at home and, as a
married woman, I could not dance with another man. But
two women could dance together, and I felt a tug at my
arm. I turned to find an aunt smiling at me. I hesitated. It
was a simple dance, but the steps were strange to me, and
I held back. "It's okay," she told me, reading my mind. "Just
listen to the drums. Don't worry if your feet don't move like
everyone else's."

We joined the dancers, entering the circle from the east,
of course. Listening to the beat of the drums, I moved in
slow, shuffling steps. Maybe I looked foolish. I bobbed. I
weaved. I tried to listen with my heart, not just my head.
Maybe I looked awkward. After a while, though, it felt right.
I danced on and on, letting the drumbeats take me over.

Some people were singing. *Heya heyaya heya.* They were
singing sounds, not words. They were singing emotions. The
drums were insistent, incessant, and I felt hypnotized, like
a woman in a trance. Moving in the circle, I too began to
sing. I was part of the circle, I was part of the music. As I
danced, I felt a new sense of belonging. Dancing on and on,
singing my emotions, I was adding to the power of a ceremony that I was forbidden to see.

My daughters giggled and counted their dollars. Some
of the young women flirted. In a corner of my mind, I was
aware of all that. But something different was happening to
me. As I danced, I was becoming part of the ceremony, and

I was beginning to understand it not just with my eyes and ears but with all of my senses and all of my body.

That night, I slept under the stars. I woke to start the second day of the ceremony, a rerun of the first. On the third day, it was our clan's turn to form a thundering posse and race toward the other camp. There were more gifts, bolts of cloth this time. And there was a candy throw, a rain of goodies hurled out of the smoke hole of the hogan. Like Halloween trick-or-treaters, the children scrambled to fill their bags with candy. The grownups were making the long ceremony sweet for the next generation. It reminded me of the Jewish tradition of teaching a young child to read the Torah. The rabbi would dab a drop of honey on the first word that the child was to read. The child would touch and taste it, discovering that learning was sweet.

I too was learning. The hard work of preparing the sheep and cooking the feast was part of the healing of a person whom I barely knew. And it was part of my own healing. My father was with me. My sisters and brothers, my aunts and cousins, were all around me. Even my sister Louva, Lora's twin, a medicine woman in Window Rock, was there. My daughters were there, and even Dickie came by for a while. Everyone was accounted for. Everyone was working toward the same goal. Everyone was there. With a sense of completeness, I remembered the prophecy. One day, my brother, my missing twin, would be there too. One day, even Brad, my missing son, might be there.

My sharp edges were disappearing. Each night, I danced again. I was part of the circle, and I was becoming part of the *Dineh*, part of the people, part of the whole.

On the fourth morning, at the first light of dawn, the *hataali* emerged from the ceremonial hogan. A tall, thin man, his eyes rimmed with soot and weariness, he stood in front of the doorway and stretched his arms to the rising sun. Then he chanted the final song, a ritual poem about the

everyday and the holy in the Navajo universe. And somehow, though I still didn't know the language, I understood.

> *House made of dawn,*
> *House made of twilight,*
> *House made of dark cloud,*
> *House made of rain,*
> *House made of pollen,*
> *House made of grasshoppers,*
> *Where the mist covers the door*
> *And the path is on the rainbow . . . .*

CHAPTER 13

In the beginning, when the Twin Hero Gods wanted to find Father Sun, they were told that he lived in the Turquoise House at the end of Rainbow Bridge. To reach him, they had to make their way past the terrible reeds, sharp as knives, and through the deep canyons whose walls could suddenly close and crush them. They had to follow a road that was lined with hidden dangers and unexpected enemies.

Old legends, told and told again, shed new light on our lives. Changing Woman gave the Twins directions, and Spider Woman provided magic weapons. On my own path to an elusive rainbow, I too needed a road map and a secret weapon against the unexpected.

"They call me White Snake," my daughter Lori was saying.

She fidgeted with her blond hair. Her voice was high-pitched and breathless, talking fast, telling things that she knew her mother didn't want to hear. We were sitting at the kitchen table, schoolwork spread over its fake formica marbling. And suddenly the path to that rainbow seemed endless and impassable.

"Sometimes," she went on, "they call me White Bitch."

"Me too," said Heather. "They call me the White Ghost of Tolani Lake."

I'd been feeling at home. I'd been thinking that we were in the place where we belonged. For months, my daughters had shrugged and told me that things were fine at school. Lori was making good grades, and Heather was more advanced than anyone else in her class. Now, suddenly, my daughters were drawing a different picture and telling me what it was really like to be half white and brand-new in a Navajo school.

"They're against me. Even the ones who are my friends are really against me," Heather said. I was deep in denial, and finding it hard to dig my way out. Navajos were famous for making up names; they seemed to have a special gene for teasing. The day before, a twenty-year-old nephew had passed me on the road. "Hey," he called out as he drove by, "you drive like an old white woman." He was grinning. He'd squeezed three gibes into one sentence, a teasing coup, a hat trick. Or that's how I wanted to think about it. I waved to show there were no hurt feelings.

"Maybe," I suggested to my daughters, "they're just teasing . . ."

"It's not teasing, Mom," Heather insisted impatiently. "It's because we're different. They mean it. Lori and I are half white and half Navajo. We're not like everyone else."

The truth began to come out on a mid-September day, when the wind was calm and the sky arched blue and cloudless. It was the day I saw red, the color of my daughter's blood. It was the day Lori came bursting through the front door, home from school, breathing hard, blue-green eyes wide and frightened. "Come quick!" she shouted. "Come quick, Mom! Heather's been hurt!"

I raced outside to see the school driver carrying my daughter off the little yellow bus. Her face was a mask of blood. She was moaning, only half-conscious, dizzy and unable to walk, her eyes out of focus. I caught my breath at the sight of her. The hot Arizona sun was beating down on the scene, but I felt very cold.

"There was a fight on the bus," the driver was telling me.

"Heather," I was saying, reaching for my daughter. "Heather, can you hear me? It's Mommy. I'm right here."

Together, the driver and I carried her into the house. "I've called the tribal police," he told me, and the patrol car pulled up right behind him. In his khaki uniform and stiff-brimmed hat, the officer assessed the scene. He held up a finger, asking my daughter to follow it with her eyes, but she couldn't. He held up two fingers, but she couldn't tell how many there were. "She needs to go to the hospital," he said, and he called on the car radio. "Could be a concussion," the Navajo officer said. "Maybe a broken nose, too." I cradled my daughter in my arms while we waited for the ambulance.

"Billy punched her," Lori told me, her face flushed with excitement, her eyes still wide with anxiety. "We were on the bus, and Billy knocked her out."

"Okay," I said. "Tell me later." Just then, the only details I wanted to hear were the ones that would have to come from a doctor. The ambulance arrived, Heather was carried on board on a stretcher, and I climbed in after her. "Get Katie," I shouted at Lori. "Tell her to follow us with her van." Lights flashing, siren screaming, the ambulance raced toward the hospital in Winslow, the same hospital I'd once disappeared from.

In the hospital emergency room, an intern did a quick

check of my daughter. A nurse cleaned the blood from her
face, then they wheeled her off for X-rays. I paced the corridor, watching the clock, watching the doors. When Katie
arrived, we sat together on a bench, and I held tightly to
her hand. A half hour passed, and I was holding so tightly
to my sister's hand that I left fingermarks. Finally, Heather
returned, walking on her own now. I let go of Katie to reach
for my daughter. She was grinning and waving. "She's
fine," the intern told me. I dared to breathe again. "No concussion," he said. "And no broken bones."

On the way home, we stopped at Denny's, where
Heather, feeling entitled, ordered the deluxe burger. There
was a bluish tinge around her right eye, the beginning of a
full-blown shiner. I waited while she enjoyed the first
ketchup-drenched bite of her burger. Then I said, "Okay,
Heather. Now I want to hear what happened." She looked
uncomfortable. "Well, Mom," she said, "I'm not sure you're
going to like this."

Factoid by factoid, the story came out. My daughters
were different. They were not the only mixed-blood children
at the school, but the others had grown up on the rez and
knew its language and its ways. My daughters came from
a different planet, a place called "off the rez." They were
the new kids in class, natural targets. As Heather now told
me, she and Lori had been teased and tormented from their
first day at Leupp Middle School. The worst of it came from
a group of bullies, mostly boys but also a couple of girls.

The teachers, mostly whites, seemed unaware of what
was happening. The bullies had threatened Heather and
Lori, warning them not to tell anyone, not teachers, not parents. The other children, afraid to say anything, fearful that
this gang of toughs would turn on them too, just stood by
and let it happen. "It was awful, Mom," Heather told me.
"I didn't call them names back. Honest, Mom. You know

how I am. I was too shy, so I tried to ignore it. I tried to stay close to my friends."

The taunts continued, growing meaner, bursting into violence on that day on the bus. Heather was turned around in her seat, joking with the boy just in back of her. Billy was a tall boy, a couple of years older than Heather, seated a few rows behind her. "He started to yell over to me," Heather said. "He was saying that I wanted to have sex with that other boy. But he didn't say it like that. He used the f-word." At that, Heather marched over to where Billy was sitting. "I told him to shut up. And Mom, I'm sorry, but I used the f-word back at him. And then he punched me. He punched me in the face."

Heather remembered falling. She may have hit her head on the metal bar on the back of the seat. When she came to, she was bleeding and dizzy, but Billy was standing over her and she could hear him saying, "Hey, you want some more of that?"

I listened and grew angry. No one had the right to talk to my daughter like that. Even if she cussed back, no one had the right to hit her. That night, I talked to the boy's mother, getting nowhere. She was a troubled woman who'd never been able to control her son. Like every other group, Navajos have their black sheep, and this was a whole household of them. The next day, I talked to the school principal. I learned that the boy, Billy, had been expelled from two other schools in the district, because of his violent behavior. I told the principal that my girls would be staying home, studying with me, until that boy was expelled from this school too. (I've changed Billy's name, to protect his privacy. He doesn't deserve it, but he was in enough trouble then, and he's walked into deeper trouble since and has been arrested.)

But there was more to the story. At home, as I kept talking with Heather and Lori, the rest of it began to emerge.

I began to hear about a school where the problems came in multiple-choice. Other children came by to check on Heather and to tell me that it was not just name-calling and teasing, mean and hurtful as those things were. And it wasn't just aimed at half-Navajos like my daughters. For all the girls at school, it was hands-on harassment.

"You walk down the hallway, and there's always someone hissing a four-letter word at you," one of Heather's friends told me. "Or there's some boy grabbing at you. They grab you on the behind. Or they touch you on the breasts. They're always trying to touch you where they're not supposed to."

"It's everybody," Heather insisted. "The younger boys copy the older ones. The other day, this little kid, a boy from kindergarten, walked up and tried to touch me on the breast."

A generation ago, Navajo boys and girls, even brothers and sisters, were kept apart and played separately. When Navajo boys were sent to boarding school, their mothers told them that if they touched a girl, they'd have to marry her. But the vices of "the dominant culture," as Navajos called the *belagaana* world, have a way of crossing over onto the reservation. Alcohol was the first—and still the worst. Others came along, like so many optional accessories on a pickup truck. Some Navajos got greedy. Some forgot about their relatives. Some lost respect.

Sexual harassment was just the latest import. It was a white-world problem. "I've got an idea," I told Dickie. To fight it, I thought we should borrow a white-world solution. "We'll sue them," I decided. "We'll sue the school for letting this happen. We'll sue them for failing to keep the children safe."

For a change, Dickie and I were in agreement. He was furious that anyone had dared to touch one of his daughters, but he was grinning now. "Yvette on the warpath," he said.

"We'll get a lawyer," I said, remembering the DNBA (*Dinebeiina Nahilna Be Agaditahe*), the Navajo legal aid service, "the ones who talk fast to help people out." Excited now, I was thinking big. "And we'll get other parents. We'll make it a class action and," talking Navajo now, "we'll be big medicine."

That afternoon, I walked down the road to the home of one of Heather's classmates. I said *"Ya'at eh,"* to the mother. There was lots of smiling and nodding and, in the Navajo way, avoiding of eye contact. We sat in silence on her old couch until, when it felt right, I began. I talked about what was going on at school. "It is bad," she agreed. She was worried about such things happening to her daughter. "It is wrong," she said.

But when I talked about a lawsuit, she looked nervous and uncomfortable. Navajos were quiet people. It was not their way to speak out or to go public. She was shaking her head. "I know how you feel," I told her, "but it's important." She sighed. "I'll make some coffee," she said, changing the subject.

"We need you," I told her, following her to the kitchen. She measured the coffee and weighed her choices. On the one hand, she was angry at the lewd words that young girls were hearing, and the indecent ways that they were being touched and grabbed. On the other hand, she had the Navajo shyness about standing out. I explained that the more parents we had in the suit, the stronger we would be. Silently, she poured the coffee. "If you join in this," I told her, "it will give us a better chance at changing things at school." She listened as I kept talking. The coffee was cold in the cup when, finally, reluctantly, she agreed to sign on.

"Will I have to speak?" she asked. "In front of other people?"

"Maybe," I said.

"I will try," she promised softly. "For my daughter, I will try."

I went from house to house, repeating that scene, pushing people to go against their natures. I was the ringleader, stirring up trouble, asking people who wanted to be silent and private to speak out. But one by one, they signed on, and my list of plaintiffs grew.

Word spread that the mothers of Tolani and nearby Leupp were uniting, and things began to change at the school. There was a school aide on the bus now, riding along to keep order. The school board held a hearing, listening to testimony about the bully who had knocked my daughter unconscious and then voting to expel him from all schools in our district.

With that, I sent my daughters back to school. Two weeks had passed, and they were restless at home, missing their friends and eager to get back to class and to normal. Heather returned to a heroine's welcome. It was three days before anyone called her "White Bitch." It was more than a week before anyone said "White Snake" to Lori. The name-calling was rarer now, and my daughters minded it less and less, but they knew they would always be different.

Meanwhile, the school board had also voted to investigate the charges of sexual harassment. "It better not be a whitewash," I thought. To make sure, I called my new friend, Thomas Atticity, Vice President of the Navajo Nation, asking him to keep an eye on the situation. As part of the investigation, the board issued a call for statements from students who were willing to step forward and talk about their experiences.

Like their mothers, the young girls were shy and reluctant. Yet they came, one after another, to tell of obscene whispers and of being pinched and grabbed. Her eyes cast down, her voice so low that it could barely be heard, one girl even named her own brother as one of the culprits who was harassing other girls. Afterward, I felt a mix of emotions. I was proud of that girl, and amazed by her courage, but I was also aware of what it had cost her to break the code and point a finger at a member of her own family.

A few boys also came forward to make statements and talk about the peer pressure that had made the harassment so widespread. "Yes, I did those things," one eleven-year-old boy admitted. "I had to. If I didn't do it, I wouldn't be one of the guys. And then I'd be the one to get picked on." A couple of fathers even stopped at my house, to apologize for their sons. "We didn't know," they said. "We are ashamed."

The teachers and the school board could no longer pretend that the problem didn't exist. They held an assembly on sexual harassment. Then, to make certain that the lesson was well learned, they set up a permanent program for ongoing education at every grade level. The mothers had won, and without having to go to court. The changes we had wanted, to keep our daughters safe, were now being made. And so, eventually, we agreed to drop the lawsuit.

Still, I felt uneasy. Victory was sweet-and-sour. I'd stirred up trouble. It led to a better, safer school for all our children. Along the way, though, I'd pushed other mothers to speak up, mothers who preferred their old cloaks of privacy. I'd pressed young girls to step forward, young girls who wanted to be silent. Some mornings, I awoke to think I'd done some good. Some nights, restless and sleepless, I wondered if I'd also done some harm.

One day at the Trading Post, as I was trying to figure out what I could afford for dinner, a shy woman tugged at my sleeve. She was one of the mothers I'd cajoled into joining the class action. "We won," she said. "We don't win too many things here. But you brought us together. It was your spirit that made it happen."

She smiled at me. "We are so grateful," she said, and it

was my turn to act like a Navajo, to lower my eyes and feel embarrassed. Once started, the quiet woman kept talking. "Everyone has a path they're supposed to follow," she was saying. "Maybe that's why you were found, after all those years. Maybe this was one of the things you were brought back to do."

"Thank you," I told her. Some of my guilt was melting away, a small floe from a big iceberg. "Thank you for saying that." For months, I'd been on the receiving end, my hand out for help. Maybe, after all, I did have something to give back to a community that had taken me in, accepted me and called me their daughter, their sister, their aunt, or "little mother."

Stanley was standing at the counter, adding up the woman's purchases, making change and not missing a word. He was the owner of the Trading Post, a newcomer to Tolani, like me, a quiet man searching on the rez for his own roots.

When the other woman left, Stanley turned to me. "Maybe it was like your weaving," he said. He was grinning, but his dark eyes were serious. "Maybe, Yvette, there's more than one way to make rain."

CHAPTER 14

A blue-black thundercloud hung in the distance over the San Francisco Peaks, looking like a child's crayon drawing of rain, with rays of it falling on Flagstaff. In the geologic bowl where Tolani sat, we were faraway spectators of the white people's weather show, watching rain fall on land that used to be ours. We were a different people with a different climate, still dry and clear when my father arrived from his ranch in faraway Kabito and parked his pickup truck in front of our new home.

No phone connected me to my father. No letters passed between us. Yet he seemed to know things in his heart and see them in his mind's eye. My father strode through the door, a great oak of a man in his jeans and his reservation hat. That day, he had a quick embrace for me, but it was Dickie whom he'd come to see.

The two men sat together for almost an hour, drinking coffee, not saying very much. Then my father came to the point of his visit. "You are suffering," he said. "Your pain is becoming worse." Dickie shifted in his chair, nodding his dark head in agreement.

Skepticism was a part of my husband's identity, like an extra whorl in his fingerprints. But he'd been on the rez for almost a year, and he'd learned not to ask how a medicine man could see the unseen or know the unspoken. "Then are you ready?" my father asked. Dickie nodded again. The men shook hands. Dickie, the nonbeliever, had finally agreed to have a healing ceremony.

It would be a simple ceremony, lasting just a couple of hours, and it required only the immediate family. Heather and Lori rode with my father. Dickie and I followed them down the washboard road to the hogan at the old ranch. Dickie had strung wires, electrifying the hogan for my father, but we did not use the lights that day. A big oil-drum heater sat on the bare earth in the center of the hogan, to keep it warm for my father, or Darlena, or whoever was spending the night there. We removed it, setting it to one side, then we built a wood fire for the ceremony.

We sat around the fire while my father chanted. He burned cedar and sage. With an eagle feather, he wafted the smoke toward Dickie. My father was chanting words that his patient didn't understand, his voice rising and falling with the ancient melodies. Dickie sat still and quiet in the circle of his family, and it didn't matter whether or not he believed. It was the being there, the being present, that counted.

My father finished with a song that Navajos believe is as old as time:

Happily I recover.
Happily I go forth.
No longer aching, may I walk.
No longer feeling pain, may I walk.
As it was long ago, may I walk.
Happily may I walk.

My father gave Dickie a piece of the sage. "Keep this with you," he told him. He gave other snippets of the sage to me and to the girls. "Carry it wherever you go," he told us. Then, as he did after every ceremony, with a bow to modern ways, he blessed the keys to our old van. "May you come and go in safety," he said.

Dickie had started the day racked with stomach and back pains, barely able to move. Now, as we walked to the van, his step seemed lighter. When he went to bed, he slept through the night. "This is nonsense," Dickie always said. "This is BS." But something happened to my ever-doubtful husband at that ceremony. Navajos believe that illness can be caused by something wrong that you've done in the past, and perhaps that ceremony had exorcised some of Dickie's old demons and restored some of his forgotten harmony.

His pains were still there, but less sharp, more bearable. For close to a month, they were just shadows of what they'd been. Then, just as the old miseries began to return, my father sensed something and sent a message via a clan relative: "Ask Dickie if he wants to have another ceremony." But my stubborn husband said no. Maybe he was being mulish. Maybe he was afraid to surrender too much of his disbelief.

Still, he continued to carry that piece of sage in his wallet, and I kept my own bit of it in my own wallet, in the celluloid window where I also kept my driver's license. I'd almost forgotten about it until the night when we were off the reservation, driving home from Winslow. Just behind us, we saw the flashing red light of a state trooper pulling us over.

"You've got no taillights," the officer told us. I was behind the wheel, and the officer asked for my driver's license. I reached into my purse for my wallet, feeling nervous, suddenly remembering the bit of sage in that celluloid window, thinking for the first time that it looked remarkably like a

bit of marijuana. I fumbled for my wallet, wondering if the
officer would be struck by that resemblance. I was worrying
now about an infraction more serious than a faulty taillight.
Dickie, aware of what was in my wallet, was as jittery as
I was.

"And may I see your registration?" the officer was saying. I handed him my wallet, with my suspiciously decorated license. Then I began to search in the glove
compartment for the registration. Without warning, feathers
began to fly out, the feathers that Dickie had been saving to
give to "those Navajos."

The officer stared. I started to explain, but he was a
fresh-faced young man, blond and blue-eyed, and he would
never understand those people from the reservation. If he
wondered about the sage, he didn't want to ask. The feathers, all over the front seat now, were enough. Shaking his
head, he wrote out the ticket and sent us on our way. We
drove off, straight-faced and silent, until we were half a
block away and it was safe to look at one another and laugh
out loud.

We were laughing more those days. We were friends
again. "As it was long ago," I thought, remembering the
words from Dickie's healing ceremony. Our truce was holding, and we had a new hope and a new glimmer of an idea
for making our lives work out on the rez.

Suddenly, I was moving back to where it all started,
back to the Internet. I'd found my family on the Internet,
and now I wanted to use it to search for something very
different. I'd gone into cyberspace to find the secrets of my
past, and now I wanted to travel there again, this time to
unlock my future.

I'd been staring at my still-empty loom, waiting impatiently for that dealer to send the word that she'd sold my
rug. She'd frowned when she first saw it. "Many mistakes,"
she said. Then she smiled. Dealers had their own ways of

making a rug more desirable. Often, to show that the rug was authentic, they told their customers a story about the person who'd woven it. And my rug came with a dramatic story. "It could bring six hundred dollars," the dealer said. "Maybe even seven hundred."

Behind the front doors of Tolani, other people were busy at their looms, their kilns, and their workbenches. My Aunt Despah wove rugs out of her history, as she said, telling her life experience through them, selling them to dealers and to individual collectors. Her daughter-in-law created sand paintings for tourists. My sister Katie's hands were forever busy, weaving rugs for sale and also hammering out beautiful silver jewelry. My cousin Irene sewed traditional velveteen blouses and skirts, and sometimes sold them. Another cousin made delicately beaded pins, and someone else turned ordinary clay into hand-fired pots and wedding pitchers.

Almost everyone I knew was involved in some traditional art or native craft. Each of us worked alone, on our own, separate little hogan-industries. Dependent on the dealers and the tourist shops in the larger cities and towns, we paid them large commissions to sell our work. I wondered about that. I flashbacked to Neponsit and Larry Silverman, trying to drum some business sense into me.

Like a Crystal Gazer, I tried to see my own future. I daydreamed about the handicrafts of Tolani, and a plan began to form in my mind. I tested it out first on Dickie. "People are making beautiful things, authentic things, right here in Tolani Lake," I said. "And they're my family. They're my clan relatives." Dickie shrugged, not sure where I was going. As I explained, my relatives were selling their crafts through dealers who weren't family, or through tourist shops that were run by strangers. "But what if I became the dealer? I could do it. What if I found the customers for them? I know I could do it. What if they sold their things through me?"

I talked about my computer, little used now, sitting on my bedroom dresser. "I could get back on the Internet," I said. For almost a year, I'd been cut off from the outside world, no phone, no faxes or instant e-mail, no messages to and from cyberspace. In that gadget-free isolation, in the stillness of Tolani, I'd looked for a new identity and a new life. But I was ready now to reach out again.

"I could sell rugs and jewelry on the Internet," I went on. Dickie listened, skeptical as always. There was the small detail of a connection, a phone line, and the deposit I'd need to put down on that, a hundred dollars that I didn't have. "Where's that coming from?" Dickie asked, his voice dry and dour. I talked about saving it up, little by little, out of our tight budget, and he heard me out. There was a long silence, minutes ticking by as he thought it over, time passing as he searched for flaws in my plan. "Maybe," he said finally. "Maybe."

In early December, the Moon of the Popping Trees, as the Indians call it, when the winter sun hung pale in the big sky, I tried the idea out on my family. They were gathered at my house in Tolani, my father, my sisters and brothers, to sign the final papers for my census number. I served up coffee and fry bread. I offered colas and chocolate brownies that Lori and Heather had made from a mix. When everyone had signed, certifying me as Minnie Bob transformed into Yvette, I started talking about the handicrafts.

"What if I went into business?" I asked. I talked about selling rugs and jewelry, wedding baskets and pottery, dreamcatchers and bead work. I was talking fast, telling a dream out loud. "What if I sold those beautiful things, from right here in Tolani? What if I did it on the Internet?"

I was selling hard, pushing my plan, but I caught an approving smile on my father's face and a glint of interest in Katie's eyes. I thought I could do it on just a small stake, just a little seed money. I talked about taking a smaller commission, so that people would be willing to give their crafts on consignment to me, rather than selling them through other stores or dealers. "I could build this business. I could spread the word," I went on, talking like someone in the movie *Field of Dreams*, "and you'll see, the people will come."

My sisters Katie and Darlena were smiling now. My brothers Pete and Robert were laughing. "You'll see," I told them, feeling a new hope, carried away with my plans. "I can reach people all over the world with my computer. I can put Tolani on the map."

I drew up a business plan and applied to the Navajo Nation for a small business loan, just five thousand dollars. I needed money to print up the brochures and flyers I was designing for mailings to potential customers. I needed to have laser prints made of my craft photographs, and I wanted to design and build a Web page for "Dineh Creations," the name I'd given to my new business.

Hoping for that loan to be approved, I made the half-day's drive to the capital at Window Rock. There, the Navajo officials told me that they were proud of their ambitious daughter, but they counseled an old tribal virtue, patience. They told me that, first, I'd have to get started on my own. I'd have to deliver the brainchild, and then they would lend me the dollars to nurture and raise it. It was a mixed message, and I felt disappointed and unsure of how to begin without money in the bank.

I began the long trip home, driving in twilight across the desert, winding my way through the mesas, moving through lengthening shadows. And then something happened. Across time and distance, I could hear the familiar voices of Neponsit. My old Grandma Sophie was telling me not to worry. She was reminding me of an old Jewish saying:

"Every baby brings its own loaf of bread." I could hear Larry Silverman's voice, talking of how he began to build his own business empire. "You start small. You make a little money. Then you put it back into the business, and you make a little more." In the here and now, I could hear a small wind whispering in my ear. "Have faith," it said. "Have hope."

Listening to the voices, I decided to push ahead. Even as I was saving for the deposit on a phone of my own, I did a trial run on the Internet. I wrapped up my computer in a blanket and hauled it to one of the rare private phones in Tolani. I plugged in the computer and slipped in a disk for America Online, the Internet service where I'd found my family. Not sure what would happen, browsing for likely bulletin boards and Web sites, I placed messages about Tolani handicrafts. That small wind was still whispering in my ear, and it seemed to be guiding my fingers on the keyboard. Answers came quickly from potential customers in California, in Ohio and New York.

"This could be it," I thought. "This could feed my family. This could keep us here in Tolani Lake."

My family was behind me, and so was most of the community. The people at the Chapter House, the same helpful people who took my phone messages, now offered me the use of the old hogan that stood nearby, empty and unused. It needed scrubbing down. It cried out for Dickie's handy way with a hammer and saw. But this traditional place was the perfect showcase for authentic Navajo crafts. It gave me a foot in both worlds. Tourists and dealers could meet me in the hogan, or find me on the Internet.

The first item to go on sale was my own rug, retrieved from the dealer who had it. Before long, it was joined by other rugs, woven by members of my own family, and then by turquoise and squash-blossom jewelry, by hand-fired pottery and handwoven wedding baskets, by framed sand paintings and silken dreamcatchers.

My clan relatives became my traveling advertisements, spreading the word wherever they went, telling everyone they met about the authentic crafts that were now on sale in Tolani Lake. One by one, new faces began to turn up in Tolani, tourists looking for bargains or collectors searching for rare items in an out-of-the-way place. With the money from the first small sales, I bought skeins of wool, strung the warp on my loom and, hopes high, got started on a new rug.

Suddenly, the Melanson household was abuzz with business talk. We'd always worked for other people. Now, we were about to be our own bosses. Some days, my head spun with the details of being an entrepreneur. Some days, Dickie had his doubts. But he was no longer grumbling about "those Navajos." More and more often, when I looked over at him, I saw something that had been so rare for so many months on the rez—my husband was smiling.

He talked less and less about leaving the reservation. He was mellowing. "It's not so bad here," he conceded. One day, as we were poring over the Internet responses to Dineh Creations, his mind wandered, his tongue slipped, and I could swear I heard him saying *"we* Navajos."

I looked up, startled. "What was that?" I asked. "What did you just say?" Dickie shook his head, on guard again, reluctant to give up his tough-guy image. "Nothing, Yvette," he said, looking sheepish. "It was nothing."

But it was something, and a few days later, it happened again. I took it as a hook on which to hang a secret hope. It was more than a year now since I'd sat in that ceremonial hogan, watching the wedding of my nephew, looking at the bride and thinking, "That could have been me. That should have been me." It had lingered in my mind. Over and over, I found myself dreaming of what it would be like to be married in the Navajo way. I never said anything about it to Dickie, but I pictured myself standing before the *hataali*. I saw myself, not quite a dewy-eyed bride, but still a middle-aged vision in bright velveteen, turquoise at my neck, a silver concha belt at my waist, carrying the wedding basket with its woven circles.

Now, with Dickie's new mellowness, I began to wonder if my *belagaana* husband, the man who was now talking about "we Navajos," would ever be willing to be a part of that picture. A few nights later, in the quiet of our little house, the girls asleep and dreaming, I sat close to Dickie on the old floral couch that we'd hauled all the way from Maine. I took a deep breath, and then I proposed remarriage to my husband of fifteen years.

"Hey, Dickie," I said, "if I asked you to marry me again, would you say yes?"

The words were familiar, the same ones that Dickie had used when he did the proposing that first, long-ago time. I wondered if he'd held his breath, as I was doing now, waiting for an answer. He was looking surprised and puzzled. Then he gave me a big grin, and he answered with the same words I'd used to him back then.

"Yeah," he said. "Sure I will. Why not?"

I was laughing, and so was he. I was crying, and his eyes were shining too with something suspiciously like tears. And then I popped the second part of the question.

"In the Navajo way?" I asked. "Will you marry me in the Navajo way?"

There was a long silence. My husband still lived with daily pain but, in this nation within a nation, in this hidden valley of Tolani, he too was finding himself. He was peeling away the anger and resentment, and rediscovering the sweet, funny, generous core of himself.

"Sure," he said finally. "Why not?"

I smothered the hard-scrabble Mainiac in hugs and

kisses. Then, coming up for air, he had something else to tell me. "We'll have some money soon," Dickie was saying, still grinning. "I'll be able to give your father those two cows that I owe him."

We didn't set a date, not yet. But from that night on, it was always there, a promise to be kept, a pledge to our future.

Meanwhile, my daughters, too, were smiling more these days. We had gone to a pow-wow, a gathering of different tribes, held on the grounds of one of the boarding schools that still exist on the rez. Those schools had been established to "civilize" the Indians; they had cut the long hair that used to be an Indian boy's pride; they had stripped the children of their native dress and punished them for speaking their native languages. A clan cousin remembered having hot oil poured down his throat because he had spoken a few Navajo words. In the 1960s, a new pride and a new spirit of independence swept through the tribes, and the schools were forced to change. Today, the boarding schools have evolved into places where native languages are taught and native traditions are encouraged.

We watched the fancy dancers in their elaborate costumes and feathered headdresses, swaying and swooping like proud eagles, and the jingle dancers in costumes hung with small metal cones, clinking and jangling as they moved, to chase away evil spirits. We saw graceful girls dancing with gorgeously colored shawls, and teenage boys dressed in fringes and feathers, stamping out rhythms. We listened to the drum groups, a half-dozen men beating a single great drum, chanting along with the insistent beat, traditional music made by men now dressed in rally caps and Nikes.

Watching along with us was a woman with hair the color of Lori's, another blond Indian. She and Lori talked for a long time, their blond heads together, the grown woman telling the young girl that there was nothing wrong with being different. When the spectators were invited to join the dancing, she and Lori entered the circle, bobbing and weaving, two birds with the same rare plumage.

On the drive home, with the mesas turning deep purple in the sunset, Lori was strangely quiet, unusually thoughtful. Finally, she spoke up. "Mom, remember what I said about dyeing my hair?" she asked. She was smoothing her hair, adjusting the barrette that held it in place, leaning over to check herself out in my rearview mirror. "Well, Mom, I think I've changed my mind," she told me. "Maybe I won't have to do that after all."

One problem solved. How many more to go? The pieces of my own life were falling into place. Who am I? Over and over, for so many years, I'd asked that question. I'd found some answers, but for a Navajo that was only half the question. For a Navajo, the complete question was: Who am I in relation to these people?

Those answers, too, were beginning to come. My sisters and brothers were different from me, and different from one another. But there was a bond between us, something that made us think and act in harmony, like a single mind, or like the fingers of a single hand. It was there almost from the start.

Two weeks after I'd arrived in Tolani, we were gathered at Katie's house, just visiting, just gossiping. Then, suddenly, we sisters were on the move. "Yes," said Katie, rising from her chair. Darlena was on her feet, saying, "Let's go." Lora was right behind them. "C'mon," she said. I was pulling on a jacket. "Okay," I said. Without another word, like a flock of instinctive birds, we were in formation. No one said "Flagstaff," but that's where we were going.

Dickie saw it happen, time and again, and laughed about it. "You all want to go one way," he said. "You get behind each other, running in circles, and then you're off.

You don't seem to know what you're doing, but then you all go and do it."

Sometimes, it was long-distance telepathy. We'd been in Tolani for six months when word came that my brother Robert, our footloose bachelor, was in the hospital. Some of us were in Winslow, some in Tolani, others in Flagstaff. Arriving from different directions, we converged on the hospital at about the same time, each of us bringing whatever was needed. One of us brought food, in case he didn't like the hospital diet; someone else brought colas; others brought his health records, his driver's license, and a fresh set of clothes to wear home. We didn't confer about it, but nothing was missing and nothing was duplicated. And by then, no one was surprised, not even me.

We found Robert propped up in a hospital bed, his usual grin in place, his long hair streaming down the front of the hospital gown. "It's nothing serious," he assured us. He smiled at the gaggle of sisters who had come to plump up his pillows, to boss the nurses and take charge of his recovery. "Who sent up the smoke signals?" he asked, teasing and laughing as always. "And Yvette, who taught you to read them?"

I was learning to be part of the whole, but I was still feeling like the weak link in the chain, the needy one, the poor-me relation with her hand always out. I was remembering the Navajo definition of an Indian-giver, someone who accepts a gift and then, some time later, gives something different, something of value, in return.

My family was still taking care of me. Katie was still showing up with bags of groceries, suggesting we cook dinner together, always bringing more food than we could eat in one night, always leaving us with supplies for the next day or two. I longed for the time when I could be a true Indian-giver, but my hands were still empty. My new enterprise, selling crafts on the Internet, could change that, but it would take time, and patience, a Navajo habit that was still new to me. I wondered when I'd have something to give back to my family, something of value. That day still seemed distant, as far away as the rain falling on Flagstaff but not on Tolani.

It was on my mind when, a few weeks later, I drove out to the sand dunes to visit the squat little house where my Aunt Carrie lived with her son, his wife and two children. Aunt Carrie was my mother's big sister, the one who had helped bring me into the world, the one who spoke the best English, the one who helped my mother talk to the hospital people about the missing twins, asking questions for which there were never any good answers. She was suffering now from diabetes, which left her mostly housebound. Her bed had been moved to the living room so that she could see out the window with the best view. The room's only other furniture was a kitchen table with three chairs and a small couch pushed up against the wall.

Propped up on pillows, with more pillows under her swollen legs, she greeted me with a warm smile. We shared news about the family. "Pete was here the other day," she told me. "And Katie came yesterday." Her smile grew wider, showing a gold tooth, like her sister Despah's. "Visitors are my best medicine," she said. She'd been there when my mother named me Minnie Bob, and she still called me that.

I answered to the name. But I wasn't Minnie Bob, and I knew now that I could never become the person she might have been. We shared a history and a census number, reactivated now. But, at my request, that number was now attached to the name of Yvette. That's who I'd always been, the tomboy with the fancy French name, the changeling who yearned to fit in, the ex-blonde with mystery roots. And that's who I still was, even if I was no longer the Yvette that Bea and Larry would recognize, no longer the Yvette that Yossi knew, or Frieda and Bob Simon, or the family and friends back in Palmyra, Maine.

"Last year," my Aunt Carrie was saying, "no one came to see me." She caught my puzzled look. "It's true, my daughter," she said. "Day after day, I sat here all alone. And then you were found and you came home." She gave me another big smile. "And now everyone comes to see me."

Her words confused me. Over and over, in my crash course on how to be a Navajo, I'd been told how important it was to look after one's relatives, to visit often and see if they needed anything. But when I asked my sister Lora about it, she understood what Aunt Carrie had been saying to me.

"She's right," Lora said. "We didn't go to see her. We didn't visit Aunt Despah much either. After our mother died, we stopped being a close family. We went our own ways, and even the sisters and brothers didn't see much of each other."

When I came home to Tolani, the relatives gathered to meet me. "Some of us hadn't seen each other for a long time," Lora told me. "You know, it's the nineties, and everyone was busy with their own lives. But then we found you, and it reminded us how important the family is. We took you around to meet everyone, and it reminded us how important all the relatives are, even the distant ones. We were so glad to see you, and we remembered how glad we used to be to see one another."

I had felt myself changing in Tolani. Now my sister was telling me that I'd also been a reason for other people to change. "You brought us closer," Lora said. My sister reached out to me. She held my hand, sun-darkened and closer now to the color of her own. "It's true. You made us a family again.

"You know, Yvette, that was a very big gift."

CHAPTER 15

A year had passed, a full cycle of Changing Woman's seasons. I was learning to live by a different calendar, marking time by the new moons, celebrating Thanksgiving from the other side of the table, the Indian side. I had the warm feeling of finally being in the right place, a boxy little house in Tolani with Bea's broken portrait still in the closet, with my loom in the living room and my computer nearby.

In my second winter on the rez, I perched on pillows in front of the loom, my fingers reaching for the warp and woof of a new rug. I was doing as my Aunt Despah had taught me, letting it come from within me, letting my fingers do the talking, telling my experiences in the threads of bright wool.

My hands moved on their own. My mind followed its own path, and I found myself dreaming of those first Navajos, those small bands of travelers, half-hidden under cloaks of animal skins, moving across continents, setting off on foot on history's longest migration. I saw them trekking across the Ice Age land bridge, leaving behind the tundra of Siberia to make their way across the frozen stretches of Alaska. Generations died during this journey, and new generations were born.

I saw them walking through Canada, crossing great mountains and plains, streaming southward. Centuries passed. They were searching for a landscape that was still a mystery, a territory they couldn't name. Instinct kept them going. Yearning kept them moving, moving, moving—until they found the land between the four mountains, the longed-for place that they could call home.

My father told a different story, the one about the Emergence. As my fingers plucked at the threads of the warp, I dreamed of that one too. I saw the First Beings moving from one underground world to another, leaving behind the dark but familiar places, emerging finally into the brilliant light of the Earth World. They walked around in circles, moving in a spiral, like the woven whorls of a wedding basket, like the fingerprints of my hand, like the double helix of DNA from which all life comes.

I saw them clearly. They created the things that now surrounded me—the four holy mountains; the sculptured buttes and high mesas; the life-giving sun, the dream-giving moon, and the diamond-bright stars. They breathed life into the first humans, and then they gave them the sacred songs, the chantways that would protect them, cure them, and bring them harmony.

It was time for my ceremony. For so many months, I had avoided it, postponed it, invented excuses for not having it. A lack of money was partly a pretext. An abundance of guilt was the real reason. I had to come to terms with my past, and I needed to feel surer about the present.

I'd been hesitating, teetering on the edge, afraid to make the great leap. The ceremony was the next step into the deep waters of being a Navajo. I'd be immersing myself in a new life, like a Jew at a *mikvah*, like a Christian at a baptism. But first, I had other people to think of. I had to know what it would mean to my daughters and to my husband.

I'd taken Heather and Lori away from everything that was familiar. I'd dragged them across the country, chattering to them about being on a great adventure, and then I'd set them down in a community where they would always be different. Heather had moaned and Lori had sulked. But then, on one of those unexpectedly beautiful days that we used to call Indian Summer back East, something important happened.

In late autumn, my daughters were invited to their first *kinaalda*, the coming of age ceremony that my sister Lora had told me about, the ritual now being held for a young clan cousin who'd just had her first period. I talked to my daughters about what it meant. "Every Navajo girl has this ceremony," I explained. "When you start to menstruate, you can have it too." I paused, and then I added, "If you want to."

Heather rolled her eyes, a typical preteen girl wondering what was wrong with her mother. "Mom, what are you saying?" she asked. "Why wouldn't I want it? I'm a Navajo, aren't I?" She was half-and-half, passionate about both her heritages, a spikey-haired girl in full charge of her own identity. She was about to turn thirteen, her own menstruation a bit late in coming, delayed perhaps by the medical problems she'd had. Lori was eleven and a half now, and thrilled with a new secret. "It's a private thing. It's just for women," she told me. "So, listen, Mom, don't say anything to Daddy." She gave a delighted, high-pitched giggle. "Men aren't supposed to know about it."

At dawn, my daughters raced along with their clan cousin, running far and fast, dropping back at the finish line so that their cousin would come in first and be assured of a long road of life. They returned to the hogan with her, watching as her mother and aunts massaged her body, listening as they told her what it means to become a woman. They pitched in, working hard to help prepare and cook the feast that was offered each night.

On the third morning of the four-day ceremony, Lori returned home, her eyes shining, her face flushed pink with excitement. "I'm not going to run anymore," she told me. And then she whispered why. "I was running along, and then I got this funny feeling, like a stomach ache. And one of the aunts told me I needed to rest. She said I might be starting my period." She caught the smile that was starting on my face and protested. "It's true, Mom," she said. "I could get it any minute now." My younger daughter was triumphant. "I'm going to beat Heather on this. I'm going to get my period first. I'm going to have a ceremony before she does."

Heather had her own ideas about that. When their clan cousin's ceremony was over, my daughters' competition began. Impatient for puberty, eager to star in their own ceremonial rites, my daughters were in a menstrual race with each other. "Mom, I think something is happening," Heather said one morning. Two days later, it was Lori's turn. "Mom, I think it's starting," she told me. Suddenly, every bodily twinge was momentous. Autumn turned to winter, full of breathless little announcements and thrilling false alarms.

My girls, their rooms still cluttered with dolls and stuffed animals, were about to come of age. They seemed delighted to be doing it on the rez. We'd been given the gift of a second horse, a mare who then presented us with a third, a foal with whom Lori spent her every spare moment. Heather shone at school, an honor student, one of a special group who were rewarded with a trip to California and a visit to Sea World, a thrilling three days during which no one called her "White Ghost." My two daughters were fitting in better than they realized, better than I had dared to hope. They joined with my sisters, urging me on to have my ceremony, excited about ceremonies of their own, already drawing up the guest lists for their own *kinaaldas*.

Dickie, as always, was a different kettle of mutton. He was the man I loved, but he was a man who distrusted happiness, biting down on it like a gold coin, sure it was counterfeit. Skepticism was still his way of being in the world. Pain was still his everyday companion, still making him grumble and complain. But again and again, his tongue slipped and I heard him say "we Navajos." He was still insisting that it was "nothing," but I added it to my collection of omens, something that bode well for the Navajo wedding we'd be having one of these days.

Hozho, the harmony I longed for, seemed within reach. The winter was waning in sun-struck days and chilly nights, and I snuggled under my Navajo blanket, still sleeping too late for Katie's taste, still missing the dawn blessing. "It's time for your ceremony," Katie kept telling me. I had a new answer for her now, a promise I meant to keep. "Soon," I said. "Very soon."

Yet each time we had that conversation, I couldn't help thinking of what that ceremony would mean to another Lost Bird, my twin brother. As I'd been told, twins are supposed to have their ceremonies together, but my brother was still missing. I knew that Katie, so eager for my ceremony, so sure of everything, such a stranger to doubts, also had a lingering misgiving about my solo ceremony. "If I have it without him," I asked her one day, "will I be taking something away from him?" Perched on our faded floral couch, Katie looked solemn. "Maybe," she admitted. Some people said that if one twin has a ceremony without the other, it could place the absent one in some danger.

Out in the desert, in the searching ceremony for my twin, we had all seen the two stars coming together, then drifting apart. "Remember that?" I asked Katie. "Maybe we should wait until they come together once again."

There was a long silence, minutes ticking by, Katie doing it the Navajo way, not answering until she had pondered the question and was sure of what she wanted to say. Finally, she stood up, shaking herself, chasing away doubts. "We've waited so long," she said. "We can't wait anymore. We have to go ahead."

I was almost ready. Pennies at a time, I had put together the deposit for that rare Tolani contrivance, a phone of my own. It sat in my "office," a corner of the bedroom where a dresser top served as the desk for my computer. With the phone now connected to my modem, "Dineh Creations" was finally online, at DinehC@Juno.com.

I was a Spider Woman, weaving her way through the World Wide Web. With the money from the first couple of sales, I went truly high-tech, buying a scanner that allowed me to feed photographs of hand-made rugs, jewelry, and other crafts into the computer and then e-mail them to prospective customers. Even before the first order arrived, I was counting the money from those future sales. It would feed my family. One day, it might even allow me to give something back to Katie, like a true Indian Giver. First, though, it would pay for my ceremony.

"We call it the Happiness Way," my sister Katie told me, explaining the special rite that I needed. It was a cleansing ceremony, and a way of being reborn. It was part of the Blessing Way, the chantway that the Holy People held when they created humankind, and it included some of the first songs that Changing Woman gave to the people. My father knew those songs but, this time, he could not sing them for me; he needed to be a participant in the ceremony, to help me in the process of being born again. He told me about another *hataali*, a singer he respected, a man who knew this chantway and agreed to perform the ceremony for me.

We set the date for early June. I began saving and Katie, the caretaker-in-chief of our Navajo family, began planning. I spent my days moving between my loom and my computer, my past and my future. In the present, I was learning to listen to the small wind that whispered in my ear. It knew my name now, but it was silent as something strange began to happen, something I still can't explain.

All along, the "Hairy One," the midwestern man who thought he was my missing brother, had refused to go away. Stubborn as desert cactus, he continued to call and write to my sister Lora, the only family member whose address he had. "You're wrong," she kept telling him. "It's a mistake." Unwilling to take no for an answer, he wrote a letter to me, in care of Lora, and she passed it along. I skimmed it, shrugged, and tossed it into a drawer.

The letter sat in that drawer for more than a year. Then, one day in late February, I spotted it on top of the dresser. I shrugged and put it back in the drawer. A few days later, I noticed it on the floor. I picked it up again, wondering which of my daughters had been rummaging in the drawer. This time, I tucked it into the drawer of a little stand next to our battered old dining table. A week later, Katie spotted the letter sitting on the table. "What's this doing here?" she wondered. Exasperated, I put the letter back in the drawer. But the letter refused to stay put. One day it was there beside my loom. Then it was between the cushions of the couch. Next it was on the table again. When I quizzed them about it, my daughters insisted they were not playing tricks on me. "It's not me," said Lora. "Me neither," said Heather.

Letters don't jump in and out of drawers by themselves. They don't move from place to place on their own. Yet somehow, for a couple of weeks, that letter kept turning up to catch my attention. When I could no longer ignore it, I sat down and reread the letter, carefully this time.

It was signed by a stranger named Dan. "I know I am

your brother," he had written. "I'm sure of it." But I was just as sure that he was wrong, and I decided that the time had come to call and tell him so. On the phone, he repeated what he'd said in the letter. "You are my sister," he said. "I know it in my heart. I've been waiting so long to talk to you."

There was something familiar in his voice, a hint of my own speech patterns, an echo of my brother Robert's deep tones, and a little sing-song lilt that's so typical of Navajos. He told me that he'd been adopted in New York and raised in a lakeside suburb near Canton, Ohio. "I was lucky," he said. "I was adopted by wonderful, loving people." They were Catholics, the religion that somehow, in my image of my brother, I'd always associated with him. His adoptive parents didn't know where he came from. "But I always knew I was a Navajo," he told me. "It was something inside me, like a stirring in my heart."

When he was four years old, according to his adoption papers, he heard something calling to him on a summer morning, just before sunrise. Still in his pajamas, carrying a toy Indian drum that had been a birthday present, he tiptoed out of the house and walked down the street. Then he stopped, looking to the southwest, "as if I were looking back, looking homeward," he told me, and began to beat the drum and to chant. *Heya neya yaya.* "No one had ever taught me that," he said. "It just came to me. It was inside me."

He kept chanting and beating the drum. "I am a Navajo," he told himself. He said it four times, the sacred Navajo number. Then his adoptive mother came rushing out. "You'd better come back inside," she said. Most people didn't have air-conditioning then, and their windows were wide open to her son's drumming and chanting. "You're waking all the neighbors," she laughed.

Dan's story sent a chill through me. Maybe it was true.

Maybe he was right about being a Navajo. There were so many stolen children back in the 1950s, and so many Lost Birds still out there. Yet I still thought he was wrong about being my twin. "Keep searching," I told him. "Maybe one day you'll find your real family." My heart went out to him and, not wanting to hurt his feelings, I agreed that we could stay in touch.

We began to exchange letters and phone calls. When I found my family, I knew nothing about Indians, but Dan had been studying Indian history and culture for most of his life. He had his own tipi and Indian regalia, and he did presentations of songs, stories, and dances at schools. He attended pow-wows and was admired for his skill as a traditional dancer. "When I danced," he told me, "I felt blessed, as if my prayer might be answered. And my prayer was always the same—to find my family."

I shared the letters with my Tolani family, but different people decoded them in different ways. I reported on the phone calls, but the details were like summer clouds, changing their shapes for different beholders.

"Could he be our brother?" Katie wondered.

"Could he be nuts?" Dickie asked.

As Dan kept insisting, he'd always known that somehow, somewhere, he had a twin. In one phone call, he talked about a dream that he'd had several times as a young boy. In the dream, he was fighting with a group of other children, outnumbered but trying to protect somebody he loved, somebody whose face he couldn't see clearly. When he awoke, heart pounding, hair matted with sweat, he was still screaming at the people in the dream. "She's not a witch!" he was shouting. "Leave her alone. She's not a witch."

As I listened to his dream, the hand that held the phone was trembling. This was something I'd almost forgotten, something I'd never told anyone, not Dickie, not my new-found sisters and brothers. But there was a period of time in my childhood in Neponsit when other kids teased me and called me "witch."

I didn't understand how Dan could know about that, but we looked more closely at his dates and places and began to find match-ups. Like me, he'd been smuggled along a route from Utah to Florida to New York. As Lora now remembered, our family had followed the stolen boy from New York to Ohio, where they lost the trail. Dan knew the name of the agency that had arranged his adoption, but the birthdate they gave him was wrong and the other information led only to blind alleys.

Bit by bit, the evidence began to mount up. "It's just coincidence," I kept telling him. "You're not my brother." One part of me wanted proof that would stand up in the white world. Another part of me was learning to think like a Navajo. I'd been living with the magic and mysteries of the rez for a year and a half by now, and I found myself moved less by factoids than by the strange stories that Dan told.

On another phone call, he hummed a song that he'd learned from some Jewish friends in high school. He knew all the Hebrew words to *"El Yiveheh Hagilil"* (God Will Go Forth to the Galilee), an Israeli folk song, a favorite with the early pioneers. Over the years, that song stayed in his mind, and he often found himself singing it. "It made me feel connected," he told me. "Deep inside, I had this sense of being a twin. When I sang that song, I had this feeling that, somewhere far away, my twin was singing it too."

Over the phone, we sang a part of the song together, Dan's voice clear and true, mine barely able to carry a tune. When I went to Israel, it was one of the first songs I learned. I sang it with my friends at Kibbutz Sa'ar, working side by side in the green fields and orchards, and then marching off to war together. Dan and I were singing together over a long-distance telephone line, but the voice I heard was dear Yossi's, singing those same words.

It was growing eerie. The coincidences were piling up. I hung up the phone, confused and unsettled. I longed to find my brother. I dreaded making a mistake and throwing my arms around the wrong man. No little wind whispered in my ear, but outside I could hear Coyote, the mischievous *yei*, howling with laughter.

Nervously, I prowled the rooms of the little house where I was building a new identity. I was Yvette, the lost child, the found woman. I was Betty and Yazzie Monroe's daughter. I was Katie and Lora's sister. I was Dickie's wife and Heather and Lori's mother. Now the last piece of the puzzle had turned up. Or had it?

"Who is that man?" I kept thinking. On the rez, I was learning to think about connections and community. "And whoever he is," I wondered, "who am I in relation to him?" For an hour, I paced back and forth, and then, finally, I dialed Dan's phone number.

"Okay," I told him. "Send another picture. Send some personal things of yours. I'll take them to a medicine man. We'll see what a Hand Trembler has to say."

CHAPTER 16

The old van had expired, sputtering and giving out after too many miles on rutted reservation roads. I was driving a different vehicle now, a second-hand Cadillac, aging and faded-pink under the dust of unpaved byways. I had tucked an eagle feather into the glove compartment, for good luck, and I was steering now to the far edge of the mesa where Calvin Nez lived in an old hogan without electricity or running water.

Calvin was a reservation patriarch, walking with a cane, but ramrod-straight and far from slowing down. He was the wise old medicine man, lean and sun-darkened, who had predicted my brother's return after just a brief meeting with me and a quick handshake. As a Hand Trembler, he had sensed it in that fleeting touch and seen it in his mind's eye. "Maybe a year and a half," he had said. As he'd explained, he was counting the moons that would wax and wane between my own homecoming and the return of my brother. That much time had passed, and now I wanted to

show the old Hand Trembler the things that a distant
stranger had sent—some eagle feathers from his pow-wow
dancing regalia and a new photograph, one in which my
would-be brother looked a bit less hairy and a touch more
Navajo than the earlier picture. His hair hung past his shoulders, the same length as mine, and it was dark brown
streaked with white, the same color that mine would be if
I weren't still performing alchemy over the bathroom sink.

"Ya'at eh," Calvin greeted me. He led me inside the
hogan, cool and dark even at midday, with only a single
window and an oil lamp to see by. We sat at a small table,
his chair facing the doorway to the east. He studied the
items, passing his hands over them, touching them lightly.
He chanted prayers. His face was impassive, with no hint
of the images he was seeing on his mind's wide-screen. I'd
been to a Hand Trembler twice before, with the personal
possessions of other possible brothers, and each time the
answer had been no.

Now there was a long silence, so deep that I could hear
my heart beating. Eyes closed, hands hovering over the
items that had come from faraway Ohio, Calvin sat in quiet
meditation. Finally, he opened his eyes and smiled at me.

"This man is your brother," he said. "The connection
is there."

I trusted Calvin and his wisdom, but I also resisted it.
"No," I kept thinking as I drove home, "it can't be true."
For my sisters, Calvin's words settled everything; the medicine man had spoken. But I was a stubborn patient, de-
manding a second opinion.

"Maybe we should do blood tests," I suggested, "so that
we can be absolutely sure."

"Maybe," my sister Katie said. "Maybe one day. But
you know, Yvette, blood tests are the white man's way,
not ours."

We agreed to find a second Hand Trembler and see what

he thought. We brought him different things—a different feather, a small gift that Dan had sent to me—but his answer was the same. "Yes," he said, "this is your brother."

"Maybe," I thought now. We went to a third Hand Trembler, and his answer was an echo of the first two. None of the Hand Tremblers knew of our visits to the others, but they all sensed the same vision as their hands fluttered over the personal possessions of a distant stranger. Even Lora, the sister who had giggled with me over the hairy man in the photograph, was convinced "Maybe the hair doesn't matter," she was saying now. She was looking at me and laughing. "Maybe some Indians are hairy, just like some others are blond."

At this point, for the first time since Dan began to call and send letters, we talked to our father about him. He didn't hesitate. "If the medicine men say he is my son," he told us, "then it is so." He looked at the photographs and saw an image of his lost son, my missing twin. His face creased into a large smile. "Now bring him home," he said.

Dan had been waiting long months for that invitation. He would come for a visit as soon as his work—a day job as a school custodian, a moonlighting career as a musician and traditional dancer—would allow. The date turned out to be June the fifth, just three days before I was set to have my cleansing ceremony.

Katie beamed at that and began to make new plans. "I'll tell the *hataali* he's coming," she said. "You can have the ceremony together, the way twins are supposed to." But I was still hesitating, still yearning for more proof, still wishing for blood tests and the ultimate evidence of DNA. My family said there was no time. "We have something better than blood tests," they said, a chorus of certainty. "We've heard from the medicine men. We've heard from three of them."

As I drove to the Flagstaff airport, my father next to me,

my daughters in the rear, I was still not certain that the man
who would step off that plane would really be my twin
brother. But then there he was, and the reality of him chased
away doubts, like a fresh wind chasing away clouds.

Our father embraced him. "Welcome home, my son," he
said. I threw my arms around him. "Welcome home, my
brother," I whispered. Did he feel my heart pounding as I
hugged him so tightly? We were twins, named by our
mother as mirror images—Minnie Bob and Bob Minnie.

From the first moment, we talked as if we had known
one another all of our lives. He was dark, though not as
dark as I had imagined, and he had the voice and the man-
nerisms of other members of my family, even a hint of my
son Brad at his sweetest. By that evening, even skeptical
Dickie was convinced. "If he's not your brother," my husband told me, "then, boy, he ought to be."

We talked late into the night, and Dan told me of a time
when he had felt downhearted and discouraged. "There's a
place by a lake that I like to go to," he said. "It's surrounded
by woods, and there's a great tree, with thick roots showing,
at the edge of the lake. I go there when I'm feeling lost or
lonely. I bend over to drink some of the cool lake water. I
kneel down there to pray."

My heart turned over. He was describing a familiar
scene, the same one I had seen in my mind's eye during my
father's searching ceremony. In the stillness of the desert, I
had sat with my family in a sacred circle, focusing all
thoughts on the missing twin, trying to look past time and
space for an image of who he was and where he was. I had
seen a man kneeling by the lakeside. My father had seen it
too. So had my sisters, my brothers, and even Dickie.

Dan couldn't remember the exact date, but he thought
that he'd been at the lake about a year and a half ago, or
close to the very time we were engaged in a ceremony in
search of him. Maybe it was coincidence. Maybe it was proof

of the power of ceremonies. I leaned over to kiss my brother, and I believed I was kissing the same man that I'd seen in the desert dream.

For the next couple of days, I showed Dan the rez I'd come to call my own—the little houses of Tolani, our mother's old ranch, Aunt Despah's outfit by the mesa. I taught him a Navajo's first lesson, his clan names. "You are *Tachii'nii*, born for *Ashiihi*," I told him. "You are Tobacco Clan, born for Salt Clan."

Then it was time for the ceremony. It was still dark when we headed for the hogan at our mother's old ranch, a caravan of pickups, minivans, and my new-old Cadillac, our headlights ghostly under a predawn sky. The medicine man waited for the first light of sunrise, and then we began. I was nervous as we entered the hogan, not sure what to expect, not certain who I'd be when I emerged four days later.

The medicine man faced east, and my brother and I sat next to him, surrounded by my father, my sisters and other brothers, my daughters, and the spirit of my husband, at home again with the flu. Dozens of other clan relatives were gathered outside, preparing the food, supporting us with their presence. On the bare earth in the center of the hogan, the medicine man built a careful pyramid of cedar wood, lighting it with a match, blowing the first flickers into the flames of a ceremonial fire. He unpacked his *jish*, arranging the eagle feathers and the talking sticks, the corn pollen and the mountain tobacco for which my clan was named.

His voice calmed me. He was calling for the Holy People to come upon us with blessings, to come to us soaring, *"with the zigzag lightning flung over your head . . . with the rainbow hanging high."* I sat cross-legged on a sheepskin, adrift on the *hataali*'s chants. The words were in a language that I still could not speak, but I knew he was retelling the story of the Emergence. And I found my own meanings in those age-old words.

I too was emerging, but I was still looking over my shoulder, still connected to another world. As my family had explained, invisible strings still bound me to the people I knew there, living and dead. My task was to cut those strings to the past. I did not need to erase memory, but I needed to separate myself from the spirits of those who had loved me and those who had hurt me.

The *hataali* chanted in a steady rhythm, and I lost myself in the rising and falling of his voice. I closed my eyes and saw Bea, the beautiful woman who wanted me to be "a lady," the loving mother I would never forget. Once again, as I did in that long-ago movie theater, I said good-bye to her. I listened to the chanting, the medicine man retelling the story of the First Beings. Behind his words, I heard another voice, Larry Silverman, the adoptive father who told me funny little stories in the days when he loved me, the same father who branded me "a liar" in the days when he turned away from me, the sad and lonely man who made those secret visits to see Brad—the boy he had once longed for, the only grandson he would ever have—for a few stolen minutes. Now, from this hogan, this place that he would find so strange, it was finally the time to reconcile, the time to forgive, and the time to say farewell.

The medicine man handed me the pipe filled with wild mountain tobacco. I drew deeply, and then I passed the pipe to my newfound twin. Within the hogan, time seemed not to exist, but the first day was ending. Relatives brought food to us, and then I drifted off to sleep. I woke to find my brother watching over me. We whispered together. He'd be leaving in a few days, returning to his Ohio family—his adoptive parents, his wife and their five children. There were some strings that he would never cut. "There are two families who love me," he said, "and whom I will always love." He hugged himself. "In that way," he said, "I am a rich man."

"Will you be back?" I asked. "Yes," he said. "Oh, yes. Perhaps my family will come with me the next time." In the dim light, I could see his smile. He was thinking of the time after that. His family had supported his search, but they were in turmoil now, struggling hard to adjust to the reality of what he'd found. He was dreaming of a still-distant time when his family would be at peace with his new identity, a faraway time when his hopes for making a home on the rez might come true.

The *hataali* was singing again, chanting the story of Changing Woman and her sons, the Twin Hero Gods. I whispered to my brother, explaining the rituals and the stories. Then I fell silent. My brother was hearing the footsteps of his future, but I was seeing the ghosts of my past.

My body felt weightless, floating on the *hataali*'s rhythm, drifting back in time. I saw Blanche, the unloving stepmother, still alive, still looking at me with angry eyes behind her designer glasses. I saw her daughter Lynn, the stepsister who pushed me away, the stepsister who didn't want to sit next to me, even at Larry's funeral, the stepsister who still lives in what was once "Yvette's house." To cut the invisible strings that still connected us, I had to slice through my own anger. If I wanted to find harmony, I had to let go of old grudges. Across the years, I wished them no harm. Across the miles, I forgave them.

Hours passed. A second day was ending. I was a restless woman, and I had wondered about sitting still for a four-day ceremony. But now, within the hogan, I felt outside of time.

The third dawn came, and the medicine man was sprinkling pollen and singing the story of corn, from which the first humans were created, on which the people had always survived. I saw Yossi, tall and suntanned in his Israeli army

uniform, smiling at me as we stood under the wedding canopy. I said *shalom*, peace to my lost love, peace to my old
kibbutz friends, peace to Israel.

The chanting continued, old stories that were now my
stories, old legends that were now my new parables for living. I had to cut the strings to old friends on the tree-lined
streets of Neponsit and in the farmhouses of Maine. I had
to say good-bye to the wonderful Frieda, the woman who
once made me her daughter, the woman who wanted to
protect me and my son with red ribbons, and to Bob, the
wounded soldier, the man I wasn't meant to marry.

Suddenly, there was silence in the hogan. The chanting
had stopped, and then there was a stir of movement. My
father was leaving. So were my brothers Pete and Robert. I
knew what was coming next—the washing of my bare body.
Dickie had railed about that. "No way you're going to take
off your clothes in front of your father," he had roared. "No
way your brothers are going to see you like that." But as
my sisters had explained, the *hataali* was the only man who
would be present for that part of the ceremony. At that
point, though, we hadn't known that my twin brother would
be there too.

The chanting began again. The medicine man poured
water into a bowl of yucca leaves, stirring the mixture into a
froth, creating the ceremonial suds. I knelt on the sheepskin,
pulling off my shirt, bare to the waist. My brother knelt next
to me. My sisters surrounded me, shielding me with a modest blanket, washing me with the water and yucca. I could
feel their hands on me, strong but loving. They were washing away the years of old hurts, old resentments, old aches.
They were cleansing me of the past. They were freeing me
of yesterday.

In my mother's time, before the days of hospitals and
maternity wards, newborn babies were washed with this
same water and yucca. When we were born, my mother

must have washed her twins in this same way. Did I cry then? I was crying now, crying quietly, crying with a happiness that took me by surprise.

In this ceremony, I was born for a second time, a second chance. It was, as my sisters had promised, a new beginning. But as they also told me, it was supposed to be followed by other ceremonies, the milestone rituals that I had missed when I was stolen away. By Navajo tradition, the one that should come next was that special ceremony, the one to celebrate my laughter.

The fire cast shadows on the walls of the hogan, the silhouettes of Yvette and Dan being reborn, the silhouettes of the sisters who were cleansing the two of us with yucca leaves, the tall shape of the medicine man chanting a welcome to an emerging Navajo. Then it was done. We were dressed again, ready for the others to return and meet their reborn daughter and sister and their rediscovered son and brother.

From sunrise to sunset, the ceremony went on. It continued through the night, songs and stories in their ordained order. For a time, I fell asleep on the sheepskin. I woke feeling refreshed, feeling revived, feeling different. I woke to a new day, the first glint of dawn coming through the hogan window. It was the fourth day, the same number of days as the four directions, the four holy mountains, the four races of the earth.

I had gone searching for my family, but I had found myself. I was discovering a new harmony. As a white woman, I had beaten my head against stone walls and broken my heart trying to change what couldn't be changed. Now I was learning the great Navajo secret—how to live in the world as it is, how to adapt, how to bend in the wind so as not to break.

I was learning what to leave behind, and what to keep with me forever. I was following a new road of life, but in the Navajo way, it ran parallel to my old Moses road. I was still a woman who looked in the rearview mirror, but I had found the switch that clicked the view from day to night, from now to then, from the glare of pursuing headlights, always there, always following, to a clearer vision.

It was lighter, brighter now in the hogan. The medicine man burned some sage and, with an eagle feather, wafted the smoke toward me. He sprinkled some corn pollen. I was surrounded by the people who created me and sustained me, my birth family and my nuclear family, and the medicine man was singing of a new world, an earth that was safe now from the old monsters.

My brother, my other half, was there, and I knew that I would always feel his spirit at my side. Across the long miles, I could sense another soul, my lost son, and I could hear his voice, a faint whisper that said, "I'm coming home, Mom. I'll be there soon."

We stood for a moment, a circle of love around the ceremonial fire. Then the medicine man opened the door of the hogan. In the glow of sunrise, he began to sing the final song:

Happily, may I walk.
Happily, with beauty before me, may I walk.
Happily, with beauty behind me, may I walk.
Happily, with beauty all around me, may I walk.
Happily, with long life, may I walk.
In beauty, it is finished.
In beauty, it is finished.
In beauty, it is finished. . . .

I followed the medicine man's footsteps, emerging from the hogan. I felt whole and complete. Arms around my daughters, I stood once again under the big, sheltering sky, a new day's sun climbing on the horizon, leaving streaks of